PULPIT AND TABLE

PULPIT
AND
TABLE

SOME CHAPTERS IN THE HISTORY OF
WORSHIP IN THE REFORMED CHURCHES

HOWARD G. HAGEMAN

Wipf & Stock
PUBLISHERS
Eugene, Oregon

Wipf and Stock Publishers
199 West 8th Avenue, Suite 3
Eugene, Oregon 97401

Pulpit and Table
By Hageman, Howard G.
Copyright©1962 by Hageman, Howard G.
ISBN: 1-59244-755-4
Publication date 7/7/2004
Previously published by John Knox Press, 1962

For Carol

FOREWORD

A church can live without worshiping no more than a man can live without breathing. Worship is the central act in the church's life, her joyful response to God's gift in Jesus Christ.

In ecumenical discussions worship has been one of the principal topics, not only because it is the common experience binding the churches together but also because its forms are bound up with many of the problems of faith and order that now divide the churches. A host of reports, monographs, and books dealing with various aspects of worship has been produced.

Nevertheless, two weaknesses may be detected in the midst of this activity. First, when worship becomes a problem, it is unmistakably clear that something is missing; the church's life has become artificial, and there is a pressing need for renewal. And, second, as with so much ecumenical discussion, the materials on worship have been limited to the few and have not been influential in congregational life.

In part this is a problem of distribution and interpretation that must be solved if the church is to receive full benefit from the Biblical and theological renewal that is taking place in many quarters today, but equally it is a product of beginning discussions of worship at the wrong end, at a level that is detached and remote from the life of the worshiping congregation.

The malaise of the church is clearly seen in the impoverished worship of congregations. Many of our churches are in this respect more "deformed" than "reformed." This deformation is reflected in low churchmanship, excessive individualism, emptied sacraments, and improvised worship. Even the sermon, long the mainstay of the Protestant service after all else had been reduced to "preliminaries," has fallen into such neglect that some are now seriously urging that it be replaced by a panel.

Dr. Hageman has presented in his Stone Lectures a perspective for dealing with this problem. He has a firm grasp of the history

7

of Reformed worship and is able to illuminate many chapters in its development from the early days in Zurich and Strasbourg to the present. He is convinced that theology must take precedence over aesthetics, psychology, and tradition in determining the response which the congregation makes to the gospel of God. But he does not write as a liturgical conformist. He is well aware that just as the genius of the Reformed tradition has been its ability to produce creeds that are concrete and particular and are relevant to different conditions and different times, so in worship this genius may be seen in the many liturgies that have developed as authentic responses to the dynamic presence and action of God in the midst of his people.

This book is written by one who, although he has served his communion at almost every level of its work, including its highest office, has remained a pastor intimately involved in the life of a congregation set in the heart of one of the nation's great cities. Through his ministry he has demonstrated the centrality of worship in the life of the congregation and the power of its witness to those outside the church.

It is hoped that these chapters in the history of Reformed worship will contribute to a renascence of congregational life, where liturgy is not confused with ritual but is understood as the service of the people of God in joyful thanksgiving for what he has done and in eager anticipation of the fulfillment of his purpose.

JAMES I. McCORD

PREFACE

When I was invited to deliver the Stone Lectures in Princeton Seminary and was asked by President Mackay to address them to some aspect of the worship of the Reformed churches, after the initial delights of flattery had passed I began to view my situation with some alarm. What could a parish minister contribute to the knowledge of this subject that had not already been explored by scholars in Britain and on the Continent?

In the last half-century, for example, the liturgical ideas of John Calvin have been the subject of such exhaustive study that it would seem impertinent to suggest any omissions and irrelevant to repeat what others have already written. The same statement could be made about studies in the liturgical history and tradition of individual Reformed churches.

But it seemed to me that at least three questions remained to be explored.

(1) Although we have excellent information about Calvin's liturgical ideas, there is not much to tell us why his ideas have had relatively little influence in the liturgical history of our churches. This question is all the more enticing when we consider Calvin's enormous influence in almost every other area of the life of the Reformed churches.

(2) I have already mentioned the many excellent national liturgical histories. But no one ever has undertaken a synoptic version of the liturgical history of the Reformed churches. The absence of such an undertaking is doubtless a good indication of its impossibility—but I intend to try it!

(3) No one has ever fully investigated the influence of what could be called the "liturgical underground" in the various Reformed churches, especially the way in which these informal lobbies influenced each other. In this connection, the considerable contribution of one of our American Reformed churches is often

overlooked by scholars across the Atlantic, even though these same contributions affected their own communions.

With these questions in the background, we shall now turn to our task. I am fully conscious that what follows represents only *chapters* in this history. Though the decision is debatable, I have, for example, excluded English Puritanism and New England Congregationalism from extended consideration in the story. I have tried to limit myself to those persons and movements which seemed to have lasting significance. To trace the full story of every liturgical movement in every Reformed church, especially in the present time, would require a volume many times the size of this one.

One final word may be added. If the story of the European Reformed churches has been told in somewhat greater detail than the British, it is because that part of the story seemed to me less well known and less readily available in English. The telling of this part of the story involves many quotations from works in another language. In all cases the translation used is my own.

H. G. H.

North Reformed Dutch Church
Newark, New Jersey

CONTENTS

I

A TALE OF TWO CITIES

There was a time when it would have come as a surprise to many persons to learn that the worship of the Reformed churches has a history. Indeed, there are probably some who still think that at the time of the Reformation all the paraphernalia of the Mass was discarded for a sermon with such simple attendant devotional exercises as seemed appropriate to the preacher. When one of the historic Reformed liturgies was presented before the national assembly of one of our largest Reformed communions a few years ago, the bewildered comments of many of the spectators clearly indicated that the words *Presbyterian* and *Liturgy* were two that they had never before put together!

It is equally disheartening to observe the ignorance of our tradition often manifested by those in traditionally liturgical churches. A surprisingly large number of their scholars are apparently unaware that liturgy is not an entirely unknown concept in our tradition but is one which, from time to time, has been the subject of considerable attention and study. That the point of view differs considerably from that of Roman, Anglican, or Lutheran liturgics is undeniable. But that difference hardly excuses the patronizing way in which these persons often refer to a subject of which evidently they know little.

It will be our purpose to record at least some of the changing concepts and influences which make up the liturgical history of the Reformed churches. Not the least part of our inquiry will be the attempt to discover why and when and how our churches lost interest in their liturgical heritage and under what auspices they began to recover it. But at the outset one or two general propositions need to be stated clearly.

Obvious as it may seem, it is worth stating that from the time of their origin the Reformed churches had a vital interest in the question of public worship. They were no less liturgical than the Lutheran or Anglican churches; they came into the world with fully defined and completely expressed orders of worship.

To be sure, in contrast with Anglican or Lutheran churches the Reformed churches were much less concerned with ceremonial, although certainly not without ceremonies. We should do well to avoid the common confusion of *liturgy* with *ceremony*. *Liturgy* is what the Christian community says, whether in speech or song, whether through itself or through its ministry, in its act of worship. *Ceremony* is the way in which it is said, the gestures, actions, settings which accompany it. From the beginning the Reformed churches, though modest in their ceremonial, were fully liturgical.

It is not hard to understand why. Called into being against the background of a church which had a fully developed liturgy and (they would have said) an overdeveloped ceremonial, ministering to a people who had come directly from that church, set in a social context in which that church surrounded it menacingly on every side, the Church of Jesus Christ Reformed according to the Word of God had to be very explicit about the content and the significance of its worship. The creation of new liturgies (and new ceremonies) to express the new way in which the gospel had found our Reformed forefathers was a task, therefore, the necessity of which was obvious.

That basic fact helps us to understand the stark way in which they believed that liturgy must be expressive of doctrine. The aesthetics of worship, the psychology of worship, the tradition of worship, were very secondary considerations with them, if indeed they were considerations at all. Their one purpose was what could be called the dogmatics of worship. Above all they wanted their liturgy to be an adequate and accurate expression of their theology, the new, or rather, the rediscovered theology of the Word of God.

Doubtless it is true that any liturgy is initially concerned with theology. But in the course of centuries liturgies tend to become encrusted with all kinds of secondary growths and acquired meanings. They tend to become independent disciplines. The older liturgies have produced the ritualist whose concern is with ceremonial correctness rather than theological content. It is this fact which accounts for the rude way in which the Reformed fathers treated the traditional liturgies. For them new theological insights demanded totally new liturgical expressions. The direct dependence of liturgy on theology is nowhere better seen than at the beginning of the Reformation. As the late Dr. van der Leeuw once said, "Whoever takes the little finger of liturgy soon discovers that he has grabbed the whole fist of theology."

There is another factor in the nature of Reformed worship which makes the telling of its story different from that of other churches. In the history of either Anglican or Lutheran worship, for example, there is one standard rite, the *Book of Common Prayer* or Luther's *Formula Missae*, with which the story begins. But the first chapter in the history of our worship is cluttered with an embarrassing proliferation of liturgies, some good, some bad, and some certainly different.

They were produced as each community tried its hand at liturgical reform, usually under the auspices of the local reformer. Many of these attempts were shortlived. Some were deservedly so, while the demise of others may be regretted since they provided a hopeful beginning for developments that never took place. Incidentally, the abundance of these early Reformed liturgies makes it very easy for anyone to prove almost any liturgical point. We must be careful not to accept too readily any statement about the liturgical mind of the Reformed church based on them. If a significant point can be demonstrated from one liturgy, its opposite can often be demonstrated from another!

But there is good reason for this liturgical abundance. It has its parallel in the fact that the Reformed churches can show almost as great a confessional abundance. Just as we have no Augsburg Confession, so we have no *Book of Common Prayer*. Just as our single devotion to the final authority of the Word of God has prevented our absolutizing any confessional document, so it has prevented any like absolutizing of a liturgical document. If anyone speaks about *the* Reformed way of worship, he is talking nonsense. There can be no such thing. The historical pattern which has emerged can be scrapped tomorrow if we find ourselves better instructed from the Word of God.

This fact is important. Not only does it account for the great variety of beginnings, the extreme fluidity of our liturgical history, but it also reminds us of the encouraging openness of our present liturgical situation. Let others lament the lack of any fixed liturgical norm or the fact that Calvin's *Liturgy* did not become our *Book of Common Prayer*. If we are Reformed we shall glory in it not because we believe in unbridled license but because of our conviction that our liturgical life has always been and still must be under the judgment and corrective of the living Word.

Out of all this confusing early evidence there do emerge two liturgical traditions which have proved historically viable in the Reformed churches. With negligible exceptions, all the worship of all the Reformed churches can be traced back to one of these two sources. One of these exceptions will be mentioned later. But even that exception is largely the result of a fusion of these two traditions which we have now to consider.

The older of them and, in some ways, the more influential, is the tradition of Zurich, a tradition which was almost the single creation of Zurich's reformer, Ulrich Zwingli. Zwingli was a man of many contradictions. In some ways he was as much a literalist as any fundamentalist; in some ways he was a Renaissance humanist; in some ways he was spiritually kin to that left wing of the Reformation which Luther characterized as *Schwärmerei*. Liturgically he was far more creative than Calvin or even than Luther. But his liturgical creativity reflected all of the contradictions of his personality.

When he came to Zurich to be preacher at the Cathedral there, Zwingli found a liturgical practice which had become common not only in southeastern Germany and the German-speaking cantons of Switzerland, but in Europe generally. Traces of the *prone* (or more technically *pronaus*) go back as far as the time of Charlemagne. The prone was a short service in the vernacular containing a variety of things but almost always a sermon on the liturgical gospel. It was usually said before Mass, though sometimes it was inserted after the reading of the gospel in Latin.

Manuals had been issued to indicate how the prone should be conducted and what it should contain. Zwingli was certainly familiar with the one published in 1506 by Ulrich Surgant, priest at St. Theodore's in Basel, where Zwingli himself had studied.

Surgant's arrangement of the prone was as follows:

> Announcement of the text
> Our Father
> Ave Maria
> Sermon
> Bidding Prayer, concluding with remembrance of the departed
> Our Father
> Ave Maria
> Apostles' Creed
> Decalogue
> General Confession and Absolution
> Conclusion—Pray God for me as I will for you in the office of the holy mass.[1]

It was in this service of the prone that Zwingli preached in Zurich from 1519 to 1523. His only change was that instead of preaching on the liturgical gospel, he preached consecutively from an entire book of the Bible, beginning in 1519 with St. Matthew's Gospel. Every Sunday and festival day saw this evangelical service in German, followed by the celebration of the Mass in Latin.

But it was obvious that this strange combination could not endure for long. Little as the congregation in Zurich might understand of the Latin Mass, it contained many things which

Zwingli found increasingly offensive. At first these objections were those common to the Reformation, centering in the idea of the Mass as a sacrifice. Luther had the same objections. The first liturgical attempts of each reformer, Zwingli's *Epicheiresis* and Luther's *Formula Missae,* appeared in the same year, 1523, though Zwingli's was earlier by a few months.

It is interesting to compare them. Both liturgies are still in Latin. Much as they emphasized preaching in the vernacular, both Zwingli and Luther were equally reluctant at first to celebrate the Sacrament in German. Both had been priests in the Latin Church; both still had a strong emotional attachment to the Latin Mass, something which Calvin, a second-generation reformer, had never experienced.

The first part of both Zwingli's and Luther's Mass is very similar. Indeed it is little changed from the Roman rite itself. Beginning with the chanted Introit, Kyrie, and Gloria in Excelsis and continuing on through the Preface and Sanctus, things are left pretty much as they had been.

In the Roman Mass, the Preface and Sanctus are followed by the Canon, a series of prayers in which the Mass is clearly presented as a sacrifice, the priest offering the bread and wine that they may become the body and blood of Christ. At this point both Luther and Zwingli took strong exception. Luther completely scrapped everything in the Canon except the Words of Institution and the Lord's Prayer. Indeed it is only recently that some of the Lutheran churches in this country have approved a new Canon to fill the hole left when Luther tore the old one out of the Mass more than four centuries ago.

Zwingli was less negative than Luther. Instead of omitting most of the Canon he wrote a substitute for it, the latinity of which is said to be far superior to that of the Mass—as we should expect from a Renaissance humanist! But the content of these four substitute prayers which make up Zwingli's new Canon will bear close examination. Though they have preserved the form, they have altered the meaning of the Mass more radically than Luther's excision. Those prayers which in the Latin Mass had offered the sacrifice have now become a petition that Thou wilt never deprive us, O Lord, of the food of Thy Word. For it is the bread which gives life to the world; in vain do we eat the flesh of Thy Son and drink His blood, unless through faith in Thy Word we believe this above all else—that our Lord Jesus Christ, crucified for us, has atoned for the sins of the whole world. For He has Himself said that the flesh profits nothing, but the Spirit makes alive.[2]

Clearly this Canon is a foreshadowing of things to come—and in two years they arrived!

But before we consider the next stage in Zwingli's liturgical development, we must briefly consider his theology of the Eucharist. Following the Reformed principle that liturgy expresses theology, we cannot understand the final liturgical work of Zwingli apart from his theology. It is true that some scholars maintain that at the time of his tragic death on the battlefield of Cappel in 1531, Zwingli was changing his ideas to resemble more nearly what were to be Calvin's. Be that as it may, in the years 1523 to 1525 that change had not begun. Back of Zwingli's theology of the Eucharist was a clear and simple philosophy which determined what that theology had to be.

The strong humanistic strain in his education, together with an equally strong strain of what later would be called Pietism, led Zwingli to a simple rejection of the sacraments as means of grace.

> A vehicle for the Spirit is not necessary. . . . Nowhere in sacred Scripture do we read that sensible things, such as the sacraments are, certainly bear the Spirit with them.[3]

Since God is Spirit, Zwingli argued, he can reveal himself only by spiritual and never by physical means. There is, therefore, only one means of grace—the preaching of the Word. Then Spirit speaks to spirit; the flesh profits nothing. As one of his recent interpreters puts it,

> God and the creation are mutually exclusive, for God is Spirit and cannot enter any earthly phenomenon. Spirit only to spirit.[4]

The trained theologian could spend much time with the implied (or overt) Manichaeanism of such a point of view. Through the centuries it has certainly bedeviled Reformed theology, as we shall have occasion to see. Cyril Richardson has summed up the Zwinglian viewpoint in these words:

> The underlying concept is that religion has to do with mind and spirit.[5]

Against this background, the debate at Marburg in 1529 is a little easier to understand. Indeed one can almost sympathize with Luther. Despite his stubborn and unimaginative clinging to words, he must have felt that Zwingli's point of view would lead straight to the *Schwärmerei*. His outlook could only result in a rejection of the sacraments, especially if they be defined in the traditional manner, "outward and visible signs of an inward and invisible grace." That they cannot be, since it has been determined *a priori* that outward physical things cannot convey spiritual reality.

But what are they then? For the New Testament clearly requires that the Lord's Supper be celebrated. Zwingli answered the question by interpreting the Supper as a meal of remembrance in which the communicant confesses that Christ has died for his sins and accepts anew his obligation to Christian fellowship. Indeed, for Zwingli the Eucharist is simply another form of preaching, the dramatic re-enactment of what on other occasions has been said from the pulpit.

All of these ideas, foreshadowed in the Latin *Epicheiresis* of 1523, came to light in Zwingli's final liturgical work, the German *Action oder Bruch des Nachtmals* of 1525. It still contains some surprising echoes of the Roman Mass. The Gloria in Excelsis is still used, though it has become a kind of gradual between the epistle and the gospel. These remain the same for every celebration, the epistle being taken from 1 Corinthians 11 and the gospel from St. John 6. There is even a bit of ceremonial preserved, in that the reader is directed to kiss the book after he has read the gospel!

There is, of course, no sermon. That belonged in the Sunday preaching service. The altar has gone, replaced by a table which is brought in only as needed. The vessels of silver and gold have been replaced by wooden cups and plates. The ministers wear no distinctive dress. The communicants do not come forward but remain seated in their places while the elements are brought to them. It is, however, still the custom to kneel for prayer.

Strangest of all, there is no music. The organs have been removed and there is no singing. The strangeness of this prohibition becomes apparent when we remember that Zwingli was well educated and gifted musically. Possibly if music other than Gregorian chant or the bawdy tunes with religious words which were then popular had been available, Zwingli would have been less rigid. But the Gloria in Excelsis, the Creed, and the Psalm after the Communion were all to be recited antiphonally. Zwingli had suggested that this antiphony be between the men and women, who sat separated in the congregation. But the Council substituted a responsive reading between the minister and his assistants, with the evident result that the congregation must have been completely silent during the service. It was not until 1598 that music was readmitted to the church in Zurich.[6]

This service was used only four times a year, on Christmas, Easter, Pentecost, and the feast of Sts. Felix and Regula, the patron saints of Zurich, September 11. At all other times the service was simply a preaching service which Zwingli had rearranged slightly from Surgant's version of the prone. This quarterly celebration of the Eucharist was deliberate on Zwingli's part. Since the preaching of the Word was the means of grace, it must have pre-eminence. The Lord's Supper, a meal of remembrance, could be limited to four celebrations a year. The divorce of Word and Sacrament, the transformation of the Sunday service into a sermon, the quarterly celebration of the Supper—these were Zwingli's deliberate design, a cultus that derived directly from his creed. In it he has left a lasting mark on the worship of all the Reformed churches.

The Sunday preaching service seems to be a series of pious though unrelated items, without any real liturgical structure. Borrowing most of it from Surgant, Zwingli made some changes, the reasons for which are not very apparent.

Bidding Prayer
Our Father (no doxology; concludes with "deliver us from evil")
Ave Maria (this surprising usage continued in Zurich till 1563!)
Sermon (presumably the chapter of which it was an exposition was read just before)
Liturgical Remembrance of those who had died during the week
Our Father
Ave Maria
Apostles' Creed
Decalogue
Brief General Confession and Assurance of Pardon

The service was entirely a monologue delivered from the pulpit, the only piece of furniture left permanently in the church.[7]

The schedule of services in Zwingli's Zurich is not without interest. Every Sunday as well as every festival day (Zwingli retained the celebration of all the major Christian festivals) there was a morning service at seven and an afternoon service at three in each of the four parishes. In addition, at eleven on Sundays there was a children's service in the Cathedral only. Daily services were held in each church at 5:00 A.M. and 8:00 P.M. Every morning at eight Zwingli conducted in the Cathedral the "Prophesying," a meeting in which a Biblical passage was discussed not only by the preacher but by members of the congregation as well. Those who think two services on Sunday and a midweek meeting an intolerable burden should consider that in Zurich a minister preached fourteen times in a week. Fortunately Zwingli thought that no service should last much beyond an hour.

Zwingli's liturgical work can be summarized in this way. He found in Zurich a vernacular prone or preaching service followed by the Latin Mass. Believing in preaching as the means of grace, he preserved the prone as the regular form of Sunday worship. Recasting the Mass as a meal of remembrance and witness, he removed it from a weekly to a quarterly usage. As Schmidt-Clausing has said, there was no Zwinglian Mass![8] It will be helpful to keep Zwingli's point of view in mind as we visit the second city which has to do with our story of liturgical beginnings.

In the free city of Strasbourg on February 16, 1524, Diebold Schwarz celebrated the first German Mass in St. John's Chapel in the Cathedral. This service took place a year before the publication of Zwingli's German *Action* and two years before that of Luther's German Mass. Schwarz's German Mass is an interesting document. Without any of the theological preconceptions which so strongly colored Zwingli's similar attempt, it is a creative attempt to rework the Roman Canon into an evangelical service.

In the next fifteen years Schwarz's Mass underwent no fewer than eighteen revisions, many of them minor. The later revisions came more and more under the influence of Martin Bucer.[9] It was the last of Bucer's revisions which was in use in Strasbourg in 1538 when a young French minister of twenty-nine, exiled from Geneva, took charge of the city's small congregation of French refugees.

John Calvin had not come to Strasbourg devoid of liturgical ideas. During his brief ministry in Geneva he had used the form of service which his older colleague there, William Farel, had instituted. Published in 1533, Farel's liturgy bore a very imposing title.

> The Manner and Fashion followed in administering Holy Baptism in the holy congregation of God and in marrying those who come to holy matrimony and to the Holy Supper of our Lord in places which God has visited with His grace and which according to His holy Word, reject what He has forbidden and hold to what He has commanded. Also the manner in which the preaching begins, continues, and ends, with the prayers and exhortations which are made for all and by all and the visitation of the sick.[10]

A very imposing title indeed for a little book of eighty-seven pages!

That long title, however, indicates the basic liturgical concept of Farel's book—"the manner in which the *preaching* begins, continues, and ends." The Sunday service is a preaching service. Farel has been to school in Zurich, adopted Zwingli's version of the prone, and simplified it. Here is his order of service.

Prayer
Our Father
Lesson and Sermon[11]
Decalogue
General Confession
Our Father
Apostles' Creed
Benediction

It will be noted that, as in Zurich, there is no music and hence no congregational participation in the service. The rubric for the sermon is perhaps worth quoting.

> The preacher reads some text fully and explains it word for word, without skipping any, using those passages which help to explain what he is expounding, but using nothing outside Holy Scripture lest he soil the pure Word of God with some human defilement, faithfully proclaiming the Word and speaking nothing but the Word of God.[12]

The Eucharistic liturgy is also a simplified version of the second half of Zwingli's *Action*. But a long didactic form has been added, concluding with a paraphrase of the old *Sursum Corda*:

> So lift up your hearts on high. Let us seek the heavenly things and the heaven where Jesus Christ is seated at the right hand of the Father, without stopping at those visible things which are corrupted by usage. With joyful hearts, in brotherly love, come all and partake of the Table of the Lord.[13]

Farel indicates that there is no particular time for the celebration of the Supper. He did not share Zwingli's regard for the festivals of the Christian year. The church should be free to determine the time and frequency of its own celebrations.

A final indication of the Zwinglian character of Farel's *Manner and Fashion* is its table of contents. It begins with baptism, followed by marriage, followed by the Supper, and then finally the preaching service. Farel was not a creative person. When he got rid of the Mass in Geneva, he looked about for the nearest model he could find. That happened to be Zwingli's usages in Zurich. Though there have been adaptations and additions, the structure of Farel's liturgy was clearly borrowed from that of Zwingli.

It was this Zwinglian liturgy, adapted by Farel, that Calvin used during his first ministry in Geneva. We really do not know what he thought of it, for Calvin was always careful to accommodate himself to existing circumstances. We can make some deductions, however, from what he had to say in 1537 in the Articles presented to the Geneva Council relative to the organization of church life.

> It would be desirable that the Holy Supper of Jesus Christ be in use at least once every Sunday when the congregation is assembled, in view of the great comfort which the faithful receive from it as well as the fruit of all sorts which it produces—the promises which are there presented to our faith, that truly we are partakers of the body and blood of Jesus Christ, His death, His life, His Spirit, and all His benefits, and the exhortations which are there made to us to acknowledge and by a confession of praise to magnify those wonderful things, the graces of God bestowed upon us, and finally to live as Christians, joined together in peace and brotherhood as members of the same body. In fact, our Lord did not institute it to be commemorated two or three times a year, but for a frequent exercise of our faith and love which the Christian congregation is to use whenever it is assembled.[14]

That passage is of capital importance. It shows clearly that during his first ministry in Geneva, Calvin was unhappy about the liturgical life of the church, especially about the divorce of Word and Sacrament. It can be construed as his critique of Zwingli's concept of the liturgy. Some have asserted that it was not until his exile in Strasbourg that Calvin gave any real attention to the liturgy. But that cannot be true if in 1537 he had already declared himself at this central point of the union of Word and Sacrament every Sunday. In the *Articles,* he had already set himself against the Zwinglian practice which Farel had established in Geneva in which Calvin ministered. When he came to Strasbourg in 1538, he came to a liturgical usage which was much more in accord with his already expressed ideas.

Despite the drastic revisions to which it had been subjected at the hands of Martin Bucer, the Strasbourg liturgy in 1538 still held to the weekly service of Word and Sacrament. Whether the prone had ever been used in that city or not, there was no trace of it in Bucer's service. His liturgy was still a recognizable evangelical version of the historic liturgy of western Christendom.

By the time of Calvin's arrival in Strasbourg, however, the weekly Eucharist continued only in the Cathedral. The weekly celebration had originally been the custom in the parish churches as well. But by 1538 there was only a monthly celebration in them. Whether this was the result of Swiss influence, whether, as Büchsenschütz seems to suggest,[15] it was the result of the stern warnings against careless communicating which Bucer had inserted into the liturgy, or whether it was simply the fact that people accustomed, despite the weekly Mass, to receive the Eucharist only occasionally could not suddenly be persuaded to receive it weekly, it was a monthly Eucharist that was celebrated in all the parish churches in Strasbourg and by Calvin in his own French congregation.

But it is important to notice the provision made by Bucer, and later by Calvin, for those Sundays when there was no celebration of the Eucharist. We do not find, as with Zwingli or Farel, two separate services, one for preaching and the other for the Eucharist. There is but one service for the Lord's Day, rubricated to show at what point and in what manner it may be terminated whenever the Eucharist is not to be celebrated. In Strasbourg we are working with a very different theological background from that in Zurich or even in Geneva. Here the Eucharist is seen as a necessary part of the cultic act, so necessary that it must determine the structure of the service even when it is not celebrated.

When asked to provide a liturgy for his small congregation of French refugees, Calvin did little more than make a translation of Bucer's liturgy. Instead of the singing of the Kyrie and Gloria in Excelsis, Calvin used the singing of the Decalogue. This custom he probably brought to Strasbourg from Geneva, where it had been read every Sunday as part of Farel's service. Each stanza of the version of the Decalogue Calvin used concluded with the Kyrie Eleison in Greek. There were some alterations in the position of the Creed and the Eucharistic prayer. Furthermore, the exhortation before the Communion was largely Calvin's own composition. But in the main, even down to small details, the service was simply a French translation of Bucer.

Recently a Dutch scholar has argued that this translation proves that Calvin had little concern about liturgy, but simply, whether in Strasbourg or Geneva, followed local custom.[16] In view of what he submitted to the Council during his first Genevan ministry, however, not to mention the way in which he tried, though vainly, to make Geneva conform to Strasbourg during his second ministry, such a contention cannot be true. If Calvin largely translated Bucer for his Strasbourg liturgy, it was because what he found in Strasbourg so largely accorded with his own liturgical preferences, preferences which, at least theoretically, he never surrendered for the rest of his life.

Before we consider his liturgy in greater detail, we can notice how it impressed a young French student in Strasbourg in 1545. Calvin, to be sure, had already returned to Geneva, but the structure of his service was unchanged.

> There is a French Church here which is attended . . . by many fine people who speak that language both from France and Italy. On Sundays (no festivals are celebrated here except Christmas) in the morning there are the so-called general prayers. . . . They sing a Psalm of David or some prayer taken from the New Testament. This is sung by everyone, men and women together in fine harmony, a wonderful thing to see. You must understand that everyone has a music book in his hand. That is how they can keep together. I never imagined that it could be as pleasant and delightful as it is. . . .
>
> Instead of the mass on Sundays they sing two psalms or prayers. After that a sermon is preached. They sing one psalm before the sermon and the other after. The first is the Ten Commandments, very well translated. If I had time, I would send you a copy. When this has been finished, the minister kneels before a wooden table, made like an altar, but not vested except when they celebrate the Holy Supper of our Lord Jesus Christ. . . . Then this altar has only a pure white cloth, without any other ornaments such as candles or other decorations. This altar is placed in the midst of the church where the minister is, as I have told you, facing the people, praying for them in their own language in a loud and clear voice which everyone understands. When he has finished praying, he goes to the pulpit and

preaches a sermon which lasts from half past seven till nine
o'clock. These sermons are wonderfully fine to hear. As I have
said before, they sing after the sermon.[17]

This letter, written by a Roman Catholic student, provides an
interesting commentary on the text of Calvin's Strasbourg liturgy,
despite some of its confusion. Evidently Calvin began with a general confession and absolution. Two things should be noticed here.
First, the description implies that the service began with a confession of sin, followed by words of assurance which the published text indicates were in reality an absolution. The second, as
we can see from examining the text of the service, is the fact that
Calvin's form is definitely an absolution, not a prayer for forgiveness.

During the singing of the Decalogue (with the Kyrie as its re-
frain) Calvin left the Table and went to the pulpit for the sermon. The singing was interrupted by a short prayer. Like Zwingli,
Calvin preached expositions on entire books of the Bible and did
not use the liturgical pericopes. Returning to the Table after the
sermon, he offered a general prayer of intercession for the magis-
trates, the church, the afflicted, etc., followed by the singing of
the Apostles' Creed. If there was to be no celebration of the
Eucharist, the service was terminated with the Aaronic blessing.

Combining Calvin's liturgy with the indications from the student's letter, we get the following result for a Sunday morning
service. Psalms which are not in the liturgy may have been sung
by the congregation. The letter seems to indicate this.

> Votum—"Our help is in the name of the Lord, etc."
> General Confession
> Absolution
> Singing of the First Six Commandments
> Short Prayer
> Singing of the Second Four Commandments
> Prayer for Blessing on the Word
> Lesson and Sermon
> Great Prayer of Intercession
> Apostles' Creed
> Blessing

If there was to be a celebration of the Eucharist, as there was once each month, during the singing of the Creed the minister prepared the elements, after which he offered a brief prayer. The narrative of institution and a long exhortation followed. To receive the sacrament the people came to the Table and knelt, receiving from the minister or his assistant. After a short prayer of thanksgiving, the service was concluded with the singing of the Nunc Dimittis and the blessing.

In all of Calvin's services, kneeling was the accepted posture for prayer, as it had been with Zwingli. All of the prayers in Calvin's liturgy were fixed prayers to be read by the minister. Only the prayer before the reading and preaching of the Word contained a place for *ex tempore* prayer as the needs of the congregation might direct. But even here Calvin provided a model.

Two comments about this Strasbourg liturgy are in order. We should strongly underscore the fact that, unlike the liturgy in Zurich or Geneva, the Strasbourg service provided for singing, something which had Calvin's enthusiastic endorsement. His liturgy is not really complete without the musical portions which gave the people their voice in the service. Those same Articles of 1537 in which, during his first Genevan ministry, Calvin had requested a weekly Eucharist had also pleaded for the introduction of singing in the liturgy.

> Another matter is the Psalms which we wish to have sung in church. . . . We cannot imagine the advancement and edification which it will produce if we have not tried it. For surely, as we know, the prayers of the faithful are so cold that it must turn us to great shame and confusion. The Psalms will be able to incite us to lift up our hearts to God and move us to zeal as well as to invoke and exalt the glory of His Name by our praises.[18]

When Calvin came to Strasbourg and found that singing was included in the liturgy there, he set himself at once to include it in his French service. A month after his arrival the French congregation was singing the Psalms from manuscript! In 1539 a slight French Psalter was published. It contained eighteen psalms and three canticles, seven of the translations being made by Calvin himself to fit tunes currently used in Strasbourg. This 1539

Psalter was the ancestor of the great Genevan Psalter of later
years, when Calvin pressed into service the poetical talent of
Marot and the musical talent of Bourgeois and Goudimel (Pales-
trina's teacher) to produce one of the lasting monuments of the
Calvinistic Reformation.

When one considers the tremendous influence of this Psalter
not only in France and Switzerland, but in the Netherlands, Hungary, and Germany as well, how it became one of the liturgical
identifications of Reformed people, to say nothing of its intrinsic
merits musically, it is melancholy to think of the complete neglect
into which it has fallen among the Calvinists of this country.
There are congregations of the Reformed Church in America, for
example, in which it is considered the badge of orthodoxy to
croon the latest picnic music from some gospel publishing house
—in the name of sound Calvinism! In these days of revived interest in Calvin's liturgy, we need a revival of interest in the most
influential part of that liturgy, the Psalter.

Something needs to be said also about the content of that long
exhortation before the Communion. In this didactic section the
creed which governs the cultus comes to clear expression. If we
ask why, in contrast to Zwingli, Calvin argued for a weekly celebration of the Eucharist, here is the answer. If for Zwingli eating
the flesh and drinking the blood of Christ meant believing that
he died for us, for Calvin it meant being inwardly united with
Christ through the power of the Holy Spirit.

An Anglican critic has called this exhortation

> . . . a liturgical monstrosity, didactic and polemical, . . .
> arguing a correct definition of the Sacrament, and going off to-
> ward the end into a controversial digression.[19]

Despite his judgment, there is a strain of Christocentric piety here
which deserves to be quoted.

> First of all, then, let us add faith to these promises which Jesus
> Christ who is Truth itself has spoken with His own lips. He
> wants to make us true partakers of His body and blood that we
> may entirely possess Him so that He may dwell in us and we in
> Him. Though we see only bread and wine, let us not doubt that

He will accomplish spiritually in our souls all that He represents to us externally by these signs. He is the heavenly bread to nourish us and to make us live eternally. So let us not be ungrateful for the infinite goodness of our Savior Who spreads all His blessings and all His riches on this Table to give them to us, since in giving Himself to us He testifies that everything which He has is ours.[20]

One wonders whether if this paragraph had been written as a prayer instead of an exhortation, it would have been found so objectionable. Certainly there is a high devotional quality here which makes it easy to see why its author felt so strongly about the necessity of a weekly celebration of this feast of love. One has only to compare it with similar statements from other sixteenth-century liturgies to see the difference.

We must now carry our story a step forward to Calvin's return to Geneva in 1541. In that city he tried to substitute his Strasbourg liturgy for the Zwinglian offices which were still in use. Above all he made a valiant effort to increase the number of celebrations of the Eucharist which, following the custom of Zurich, was quarterly. In the latter effort he failed, although, as is well known, he continued his protest to the end of his life. The will of the Geneva Council prevailed and Calvin had to be content with hoping for better things from his successors.

He was somewhat more successful, however, with the liturgical substitution. The Genevan liturgy of 1542, and still more that of 1545, bears a striking resemblance to Calvin's Strasbourg rite, especially when one compares it with Farel's *Manner and Fashion* which had been in use previously. The only changes are the omission of the singing of the Decalogue (a psalm being used in its place) and the dropping of the Absolution after the Confession.

So far as the first omission is concerned, we have no indication that Calvin had any feeling about it. Probably the larger number of available psalms was the reason for it. Because of that he may even have desired it. The omission of the Absolution was something to which he consented after mild protest.

That some word of promise should be added to the general confession to awaken sinners to the hope of forgiveness and re-

demption everyone recognizes. And originally I wanted to introduce this usage [in Geneva]. But since some fear arose because
of its novelty, I readily abandoned it and it was removed. It is
not now opportune to make any change since there are many
[in the congregation] who begin to rise even before we have
come to the end of the general confession.[21]

With these omissions and a few minor stylistic changes, the
liturgy of Strasbourg became the liturgy of Geneva. Although a
few churches continued to use the older Strasbourg form, the
Genevan rite became the accepted one in almost all the French-
speaking Reformed churches. Even more significantly for English-
speaking people, under John Knox it became the accepted pattern of worship for the Scottish Church until it was displaced by
the Westminster Directory in the middle of the seventeenth century.

August Ebrard, one of the nineteenth-century pioneers in the
study of Reformed worship, claims that there was still a third
type of Reformed liturgy which he called Melanchthonian.[22] The
term seems inaccurate when we consider that the influence of
Melanchthon on the liturgy in question was at best a remote one.
Indeed it can be asked whether this liturgy is really one of the
original Reformed liturgies despite its great influence in some
sections of the Reformed Church.

Ebrard's reference was to the liturgy drawn up in Heidelberg
in 1563 as part of a new church order for the Palatinate. The
authors, Ursinus and Olevianus, also the authors of the celebrated
Heidelberg Catechism, did make use of some Lutheran texts and
customs as well as some things from both Calvin and Zwingli. The
Elector who had ordered the work was anxious to end the strife
between Lutheran and Reformed in his domain. Catechism and
Liturgy alike were composed with this end in view. They represent therefore a blending of texts and traditions, as evidenced,
among other things, by the retention of the pericopes or liturgical
lessons for each Sunday. This was the only Reformed liturgy to
retain this custom, the others all preferring the use of *lectio con-
tinua*, the consecutive reading of the chapters of a given book on
successive Sundays.[23]

The Palatinate Liturgy attained a wide use in the Reformed

parts of Germany and in 1566 was in large measure translated into Dutch by Peter Dathenus. His translation, made for the Dutch refugees in the Palatine city of Frankenthal, became the basis for the official liturgy of the Reformed Church in the Netherlands. It thus became the only sixteenth-century liturgy to be used on this continent, both by the German Reformed churches in Pennsylvania and the Dutch churches in New York and New Jersey.

It is, in fact, still the official liturgy, with some modification, of the Reformed Church in America. It could hastily be characterized as Zwinglian in structure, Calvinist in content, with some Lutheran overtones. Though much of the text is drawn from Calvin, the basic outline of a preaching service with a separate Eucharist for occasional usage is Zwinglian.

And there is the tale of two cities which composes the first chapter in the history of the worship of the Reformed churches. But there are some conclusions to be drawn from it.

The theology of the Reformed churches makes much of Calvin and relatively little of Zwingli. But if we admit that liturgy is one of the most commonly experienced forms of theology, we must revise our point of view somewhat. To whatever extent theology is shaped by liturgy, to that extent Zurich has been of greater influence than either Strasbourg or Geneva. Though the use of the Zurich rite has been technically confined to a small corner of Switzerland (where it continues, almost unaltered, to this day), its basic point of view became enormously influential throughout the length and breadth of Reformed Christendom.

When Calvin came to Geneva five years after Zwingli's death, the Zurich point of view was so firmly entrenched there that it bitterly resisted all of Calvin's efforts to change it. And that hold has been such a persistent one that in the average Reformed or Presbyterian congregation today, customary liturgical practice is that of Zwingli in Zurich, not that of Calvin in Strasbourg.

Visit such a congregation next Sunday and you will in most instances discover a Sunday preaching service in which the elements are more or less strung together without any structural relatedness. Four times a year a Communion service is added which, whatever the confessional standards may say, is generally thought of as an act of remembrance. Indeed, except for some sections of the French churches, it is only recently that Calvin's liturgical ideas have even been considered. So completely did Zwingli prevail, even though the victory has not always been recognized. Know it or not, down to relatively recent times the Reformed churches have, practically speaking, acknowledged Zwingli as their liturgical master.

Part of the reason for this situation is doubtless the fact that the Zwinglian pattern was the older. Before Calvin came on the scene it had already begun to take root. In Geneva, for example, it was basically the Zwinglian idea of worship which Calvin was seeking to reform both before and after his exile. Despite Zwingli's early death, Zurich continued to be a powerful influence in the training of Reformed leadership for many years to come.

Part of the reason for this situation is also to be found in the fact that the Reformed churches, standing between Lutheranism and the freer usages of the Anabaptists, always were torn liturgically. If Calvin's ideas were more congenial to the Lutherans who were attracted into the Reformed camp (and there were some), Zwingli's had a stronger appeal to the Anabaptist mind. In a number of places circumstances conspired to make them more numerous.

Whatever the reasons, even those churches which were avowedly Calvinist in their theology became practically Zwinglian in their liturgical and sacramental life. This tendency became even more apparent in the eighteenth century when the humanistic strain in Zwingli's thought found wide appeal. So far did this neglect of Calvin's liturgical ideas extend that so careful a liturgical historian as the Dutch scholar, Mensinga, could remark with some surprise in his discussion of Calvin's service book,

> The location of the Communion liturgy, not next to Baptism, but immediately after the liturgy for Sunday morning, is remarkable. It is a hangover from the old idea of the mass that Communion should be celebrated every Sunday.[24]

It has sometimes been asserted that the typical Sunday service of the Reformed Church is nothing but a carrying out to a logical conclusion of a pattern which Calvin lacked either the courage or the understanding to complete. But that assertion will scarcely bear the scrutiny of history. Actually it was the more radical pattern of Zwingli which came first. Calvin's liturgy could be interpreted as an attempt to carry the worship of the Reformed churches back to the historic pattern of Christendom. If there is a lingering medievalism in his liturgical work, it was deliberate.

Because Zwingli used so many of the traditional elements and ceremonies, it is easy to think of him as the more conservative liturgically. But though he did preserve many of these things, he completely demolished the traditional liturgical structure. Calvin almost entirely abandoned the traditional elements and ceremonies. But he carefully preserved the traditional shape of the liturgy.

In a real sense the liturgical task of the Reformed churches today is the reconciliation of the two cities, reuniting elements and shape in a significant and integral liturgy.

II

INTO THE SHADOWS

If there is any piece of unexplored territory in the history of the Reformed churches, it is the story of the age which began with the closing of the Westminster Assembly of Divines and ended with the advent of Schleiermacher. That century and a half remains the dark age of Reformed Protestantism.

There is a variety of reasons for our neglect. For one thing, it seems to have been an age of uninviting scholastic sterility, punctuated by such resounding Latinized names as Witsius, Wollebius, Voetius, Cocceius, Amesius, etc. Who would spend long hours turning their yellowed pages when the same age affords us the exciting exploits of the Wesleys or the intricate and subtle reasonings of Jonathan Edwards?

Furthermore, this was the age which also saw the beginnings of our own ecclesiastical and theological history on this side of the Atlantic. That fact means that our attention is more likely to be focused on what was happening in the Reformed churches in America than on what was happening in those same churches in Britain and Europe.

Yet it was precisely this age which saw the formation of many of the liturgical attitudes and practices which are still current in our churches. Indeed, since this was the age in which most of the liturgical patterns that separate us from the Reformation came into being, it is an era that requires close examination. Too many of the liturgical handbooks and histories pass almost directly from the Reformation to the revivals of the nineteenth century. But we cannot understand the situation faced by the restorers if we do not understand what had happened between the Reformation and their time. Indeed, it would not be too much to say that we cannot understand the service that will be held in the First Presbyterian Church next Sunday if we do not understand the liturgical developments of the Reformed churches in this dark age. And once again, in lifting the lid of the liturgical box, we shall release a whole swarm of theological hornets!

At the beginning of this post-Reformation era all of the Reformed churches had a firm and fixed liturgical life. Scotland or Switzerland, Heidelberg or the Hague all reveal the same thing— a fixed Reformed liturgy used without variation or exception not only for the celebration of the sacraments but for ordinary Sunday worship as well. The Zwinglian divorce of Word and Sacrament had already been established as the almost universal pattern for Reformed worship. But both Word and Sacrament were celebrated in a liturgical setting. At the end of the sixteenth century there was no liberty of liturgical choice anywhere in the Reformed churches.

To be sure, the sermon and the lesson which preceded it were variables, the choice of which was usually left to the minister. The choice of the psalms to be sung also afforded some opportunity for variety. Most contemporary evidence, however, indicates that the repertory of the average congregation then was even smaller than it is now. The variety, therefore, may have been more apparent than real. But with these exceptions, everything else, including the confession and the prayers before and after the sermon, was read from the same text Sunday after Sunday.

Such a practice must have been monotonous to a degree. None of the Reformed churches at this time had a prayer book with materials for worship. There were no variables, as in the Roman, Anglican, or Lutheran liturgies, to bring changes in emphasis to the invariable parts of the liturgy which followed the seasons of the Christian year. The only possible variation in the prayers (and there is some evidence that it was used) was the use on

Sundays of the prayers designated for the weekday services.
With that slight exception, the liturgical part of the service
never changed for fifty-two Sundays in the year. The experience
of Geneva is fairly typical. It was not until 1724 that special
prayers for Christmas and New Year's Day were introduced into
the liturgy, though these days had been observed since Calvin's
time. Good Friday was not given liturgical recognition till 1828,
while it was 1868 before prayers for Easter and Pentecost became
part of the Genevan rite.[1]

Calvin and the other reformers had always left room in the
liturgies for adaptations of liturgical prayer to special needs and
circumstances. But during the first century or so after the Reformation, little use seems to have been made of this provision.
Under the pressures of the political and international situation,
in many instances under the hostile scrutiny of the Roman or
Lutheran communions, a cautious liturgical conservatism seemed
the best course for the Reformed churches.

Does this liturgical poverty indicate, as some have suggested,
that congregations in this time were not really very interested in
the liturgy? Since their real concern was with the sermon, it is
said, they simply endured the monotonous repetition of the liturgical prayers Sunday after Sunday. There is probably an element
of truth in this assertion. But there is also evidence that in at least
the French churches the confession of sin came to have meaning
enough to be cherished as a real part of corporate worship. Long
after the other liturgical prayers had ceased to be used, it was
continued, even in the experience of the churches of the Desert
after the revocation of the Edict of Nantes.

Despite the obvious disadvantages of this liturgical situation,
it had one solid virtue. The worship of these congregations was
undeniably corporate. The prayers of the service were common
prayers in the truest sense of the word. There was no trace of that
vicious practice of later years in which the prayers became the
peculiar preserve of the minister, who often abused them to
wrestle with his own theological problems, to scold the people
from behind the Lord's back, or to summarize succinctly the
points of his sermon.

At this time such conduct would have been condemned not only as display but as sheer priestliness of the kind that the Reformation had tried to be rid of once and for all. We cannot emphasize too strongly the fact that freedom of prayer, which in later years came to be considered (and in some circles is still) the liturgical hallmark of true Reformed worship, was unheard of in any Reformed church until well into the seventeenth century.

Not only were the Sunday and weekday prayers bound up in the Psalter which every parishioner owned and used, but there is good evidence that they were part of the contemporary program of Christian education. One of the ablest ministers to labor in the Dutch Church in this country in colonial days was Domine Henry Selyns. (He used, incidentally, to correspond with Cotton Mather in Latin.) Selyns served the congregation in New York from 1682 to 1701. On September 14, 1698, he wrote a letter to the Classis of Amsterdam giving a detailed report of the exercises held in connection with the reception of catechumens in that year. These exercises had been held on the second day of Easter, Ascension Day, and the second day of Pentecost. They had to be divided since there was a large class of sixty-five, each member of which had to recite from memory.

After giving a little account of what each catechumen had done, Selyns concluded his letter with this memorandum.

> After my prayer and address, our regular Sunday-prayer which is made before the sermon, was recited without any mistake, and with energy and manly confidence, by Marycke Popinga, a child of five years. It was then repeated, not without tears, by my church members. In testimony whereof this has been signed, at the request of my Catechumens, at New York, the 14th of September, 1698. By order of' my Consistory, Henry Selyns, Minister at New York.[2]

What is striking about this incidental insight into the ecclesiastical life of the new world is not only the evident persistence of liturgical prayer as late as 1698. Even more significant is the fact that these prayers were part of Christian instruction and so were part of the religious emotions and associations of the congregation. The church members who recited that prayer when Marycke

Popinga had finished, and recited it "not without tears," were voicing something which was an integral part of their religious experience.

Attention should be directed to the fact that here in New York at the end of the seventeenth century the life of the Reformed Church was liturgical. The liturgy was used for Sunday worship and weekday instruction. The Christian year was still observed with services not only on Easter and Whitsunday, but on Easter Monday and Whitmonday as well. In the light of such records the prejudice of a recent Lutheran author is apparent when he laments that

> the strongest Lutheran settlements were made in soil thoroughly uncongenial to liturgical worship . . . among the Dutch Reformed of New York.[3]

But the demerits of the system finally led to its ruin. A former church history teacher used to say, "A hundred years then was as long as a hundred years now." What had conveyed the theological convictions and religious aspirations of a congregation in 1565 was no longer an adequate vehicle for them in 1665. But just as this age was marked by theological scholasticism it was also marked by liturgical scholasticism. Synodical records of the era never even suggest the need for liturgical revision or amplification. Like the confessional standards, the liturgical forms became embalmed. One could comment upon them, discuss them, exegete them, but one could not change them.

Thus, for example, in the synodical records of the Dutch Church during the seventeenth century there are discussions about the meaning of certain phrases in the baptismal liturgy. There is even a sharp disagreement about the order of priority in prayers for the state centering in the question whether provincial or national leaders should be prayed for first. But the outcome of these discussions is always the same. There is to be no change. Never is there any effort to examine what new theological situations might lie behind the discussion.

Such an attitude, of course, was profoundly unreformed. If there was any one liturgical principle which the reformers had made clear, it was that the *semper reformanda*, which they had everywhere proclaimed as the mark of a true Reformed church, was especially applicable in the matter of public worship. The embalming of a liturgical form, no matter how ancient or orthodox, was one of the very things against which the reformers had protested. But now their spiritual descendants were guilty of the same practice.

The first break in liturgical scholasticism, and it was a violent one, came in the Church of Scotland. Since the time of the Scottish Reformation the Church had used John Knox's *Book of Common Order*, a Scottish derivative of Calvin's Genevan rite. The Scottish Church was thus one of the few Reformed churches that was faithful to the Calvinist concept of the liturgy and had rejected the Zwinglian.

The violence and speed with which the liturgical situation changed in Scotland, in contrast with the continent, were occasioned by the close relationship between Scottish liturgical and political history. It was by royal decree that the use of the *Book of Common Order* came to an end on July 23, 1637. Charles I, anxious for a religious as well as a royal union of the two kingdoms of England and Scotland, ordered the Scottish Church as of that date to begin using the new Scottish Prayer Book, prepared largely by Bishop Wedderburn of Dunblane, though known to history as *Laud's Liturgy*. (1637 was during the period of the "First Episcopacy" in Scotland, a rather uneasy combination of episcopacy and presbyterianism.)

The explosion which followed is too famous to require comment. Historians doubt that Jennie Geddes ever flung her milkstool at the dean's head in St. Giles' in Edinburgh as she cried, "Who dares say mass in my lug?" But there were well organized riots and protests which finally swept away not only the new book but episcopacy as well. It could be argued that they finally swept away the royal throne itself. But it should be pointed out that these protests were not, as so many misinformed Presbyterians assume, against the use of a liturgy. They were protests against the replacement of their own Scots liturgy by a book from England, foisted on them without their consultation or approval.

In the period of chaos which followed, some congregations used the old *Book of Common Order* while others did what seemed right in their own eyes. Various adaptations of the English Prayer Book seem to have been used in some places. But on the part of most there was an increasing fancy for the liturgical customs of the English Puritans south of the Tweed.

This period of chaos came to an end in 1645 with Scottish acceptance of the *Westminster Directory*, an English Puritan production in the making of which a handful of Scottish Presbyterians had shared. The late Walter Lowrie once described the *Westminster Directory* as the only liturgy in Christendom to consist of nothing but rubrics. That criticism is essentially true. Though each act of worship is minutely indicated and described, no text was provided for the prayers or for any part of the services. It must be said that the indications of the *Directory* were generally excellent, scrupulously faithful to the Calvinist structure of worship. The Scottish commissioners at Westminster doubtless saw to that. The absence of any text was, of course, a concession to the dominant English Puritan mind which had already become convinced of the spirituality of free prayers and the lifelessness of liturgical ones.

To this day the *Directory* remains the standard of worship not only for the Church of Scotland but for most English-speaking Presbyterian churches as well. The various *Books of Common Order* issued by Presbyterian churches in this century simply provide the text and prayers with which the *Directory's* scheme may be filled out. And, still guarding the old principle of English Puritanism, they provide them simply as models, not as requirements. When the Presbyterian churches in this country recently set about liturgical revision, their first step, and properly so, was a revision of the *Directory*, for it is still the document of liturgical force in Presbyterianism.

But it does not seem to have been in force very long in Scotland. In his excellent Baird Lectures, *A History of Worship in the Church of Scotland*, Dr. Maxwell indicates that the *Directory's* provisions were soon ignored, if indeed they were ever widely observed during the years of ecclesiastical strife which followed in that country. By the close of the seventeenth century the liturgy had entirely ceased to be a living thing in the Scottish Kirk. The coveted freedom of Puritanism became the established order. British Presbyterianism (for the story in English Presbyterianism did not differ greatly from that in Scotland) was the first in the Reformed family to lose the liturgy. One can almost feel the pained surprise in Ebrard's *Reformirtes Kirchenbuch*, written in 1847 as a general survey of Reformed liturgies.

> Incidentally I must observe here that the Scottish Church has no liturgical forms, not even for Baptism and the Lord's Supper. Everything is left to the freedom of the minister. The Church festivals have also disappeared. Only Sunday is retained.[4]

But if the Scottish Church completely lost its liturgical inheritance after 1645 (the Christian year had never been officially observed in the Scottish Kirk), the Scottish story was simply an accelerated version of what was beginning to happen in the continental Reformed churches generally and for the same reason. For what really led to the disuse of the liturgy in Scotland was not the political disturbances of the civil war. It was the spread of English Puritan ideas which the civil war greatly hastened and furthered.

These same Puritan ideas had their near counterpart in the continental Reformed churches, where they were known as *Pietism*. The origins of this movement are not easy to define, nor was it really an organized movement. Pietism was a way of thinking which spread widely through the continental Reformed churches in the seventeenth century and from them into Lutheranism.

Its origin may well have been in that same English Puritanism which had such a devastating effect on the liturgical life of the Scottish Kirk. During the troubled years of the seventeenth century many of the English Puritans and Separatists took refuge in Europe, especially, as we know from our American history, in the Netherlands. There is good evidence that when they left Holland for either old or new England, many of their ideas remained behind them.

Indeed there were parts of Holland in which these ideas found congenial listeners. Mensinga, the standard historian of the Dutch liturgy, says that the Dutch Church, an expression of the national feeling against Spain, had in the sixteenth century attracted many persons whose previous religious point of view had been Mennonite. (The Mennonites, an Anabaptist group, were so called from the name of their leader, Menno Simons.) Their center was the province of Zeeland and the town of Middleburg. Geographically this is about as close to Britain as it is possible to get.

> . . . It is undoubtedly true that however strongly the Synods may have pronounced for the use of the liturgy, in many places popular opinion was against it, partly because of the . . . Waldensian or Mennonite principle of freedom which remained strong; partly because of the rejection of anything that had the slightest trace of Romanism or Lutheranism about it; and finally because the warmth of free prayer suited the feelings of these people better than the colder, though more solemn, tone of the liturgical prayers.
>
> Gradually the attempt was made, especially in Zeeland, to omit everything from the liturgical prayers that was less acceptable or agreeable and to add to them whatever was thought necessary. This was followed by the omission of all liturgical prayers, especially the one before the sermon, with only the use of the Lord's Prayer at the conclusion. The result was that in Middleburg in the first half of the seventeenth century in the week-day services only the *votum* [Our help is in the Name of the Lord Who made heaven and earth—the opening words of the service] remained.[5]

It is not surprising, therefore, that it was in Middleburg that the first avowedly pietist congregation was formed in Europe. Although the environment was congenial in the Netherlands, as evidenced by the thinking of such Dutch religious leaders as Lodensteijn and Voetius, and the English Puritan diaspora, a noticeable element in Zeeland, had furthered it, it was Jean de Labadie, one of the most interesting characters in post-Reformation history, who first began rigorous pietistic practices in his ministry in Middleburg.

A former Roman Catholic priest of Jansenist leanings, Labadie came to Middleburg after a sensational ministry in Geneva. Some of his methods we take for granted today. For example, he introduced the custom of house-to-house visitation, a thing unheard of in Reformed circles before that. His preaching was warmly personal and not at all like the impersonal doctrinal expositions which were characteristic of the Reformed pulpit. But most significantly he brought into the Reformed Church something which is still with us—the Puritan notion that the church is composed not of the baptized but of the regenerate. Not the baptized community but the born-again Christian is the basis of the church.

Once this premise had been granted, it followed that sharp distinctions had to be made in the congregation between mere worldly professors and the truly saved. Only these latter, a kind of spiritual elite within the larger body, were entitled to Communion. Prayer meetings, religious conventicles, district gatherings, and all the rest were soon the order of the day in Middleburg.

By 1670 tensions had mounted to the point that Labadie was removed from his office by the ecclesiastical authorities. With a large number of his congregation he migrated to the German town of Herford where a Stuart princess became his great benefactress. But his ideas had taken such root that for many years to come in Holland a pietist was known as a Labadaist. So threatening did his movement seem that the Synod of North Holland, which, as Mensinga tells us, had a strong liturgical party (the Classis of Amsterdam, responsible for the life of the church in America, was in this Synod), for many years had as a regular item in its docket "Labadaism," with a watchdog committee to report any traces of pietism within the Synod's bounds.

The theological historian can trace the way in which these new ideas infiltrated their way into Reformed theology until today they have almost complete possession of those very circles which most pride themselves on their Reformed orthodoxy. But so far as the liturgy is concerned, it is sufficient to point out that the liturgy was always one of pietism's first victims. For one thing, liturgical forms did not fit pietist theories. As Mensinga points out,

> It began to be said; we cannot pray so generally for all men (as the liturgy does) nor can we so completely forget that among those who pray there are unconverted and damned.[6]

Such things soon began to be said in public. In 1674 one of Labadie's disciples, Domine Jacob Koelman, published his "Points of Necessary Reformation in the church and her affairs and among the members of the Reformed Church of the Netherlands." One of the most trenchant chapters was entitled "The Need of Reformation regarding the use of the Liturgy." Koelman's thesis was that since the regenerate man has been adopted as a child of God, he should speak to God naturally and from his own heart, not hiding behind someone else's words. Liturgical prayer could be said by anyone, even by the unconverted. And, as every pietist knew, there were many unregenerate and unconverted persons in the ministry. The only way to detect them was to strip away the liturgical props and let them be seen by their congregations for what they were.

A recent South African exponent of Koelman puts it in this way:

> The person who makes use of fixed forms of prayer only betrays that he does not possess the true spirit of sonship and actually does not have the right to pray. A fixed form of prayer gives rise to hypocrisy because the person who prays it appropriates to himself a language of prayer that witnesses against his own moral and religious life. On the other hand, the truly regenerate, having thoroughly examined himself, is assured of his sonship. His prayer is expressed out of sincerity of heart, whereas the use of a fixed form of prayer testifies to a spiritual deadness which lacks true self-examination and a real seeking of God.[7]

Koelman and his sympathizers simply felt that they were carrying the good Calvinistic principle of the *semper reformanda* into an area where a good deal of what Koelman called "Romish yeast" was still at work leavening the lump. The removal of all liturgical forms struck him as nothing but the logical continuance of the movement which Calvin had begun but which circumstances had prevented him from completing. In rejecting the liturgy he was only returning to that apostolic simplicity which had been the avowed intention of all the reformers.

His violent language caused his deposition from the ministry. But despite the watchfulness of the committee of the Synod of North Holland, Koelman's views spread. Although the sacramental forms were untouched, the use of liturgical prayers increasingly waned. The lifeless orthodoxy of the traditional party was no match for the fervor of the pietists.

Some idea of the extent of their victory in the Dutch Church can be gathered from Ravestein, although his testimony is somewhat prejudiced since he was himself a pietist. In 1743 he wrote:

> No liturgical prayer is used in respectable congregations except by a few of the older ministers out of attachment to the old forms or from laziness—and then only at Catechism services.[8]

In fact, by the mid-eighteenth century free prayer had become not only the accepted rule but the standard by which the ability and religious zeal of the ministry were judged. If a minister could not pray freely and movingly for at least half an hour, he was clearly not right with God. That is the assertion of Willem Schortinghuis, another Dutch pietist of the eighteenth century. Whoever fails the test, he wrote, belongs to the

> poor, rutted, book, head, and brain prayers who either from a dumb liturgy or prayerbook or with their own manufactured formula chatter to the Lord in a cold voice.[9]

The evidence of a Ravestein or a Schortinghuis may be prejudiced. The best proof that free prayer, *ex suo et ex pectore,* had come to be the order of the day in the Dutch Church is to be found in the regulations of that church when it was re-established in 1817 after the Napoleonic occupation of Holland. There was some debate about revising the liturgy. But the final decision was to leave it alone with no emendation or alteration. The reason for the decision was the following:

> Obviously the liturgical forms were established for the use of ministers who were not properly practiced in all the parts of their holy service and so had need of certain directions to be guided in a fitting and uniform conduct of worship. That need no longer exists.[10]

That decision should be compared with one made more than two centuries earlier, in 1580, when the Synod met in Dort:

> We deem it entirely necessary that everyone abide by the

form of prayers both before and after the sermon as it is given in
the Catechism and that no one utter or compose prayers of his
own.[11]

Admittedly there are other milder statements from other early
Dutch Synods. But in two centuries the Dutch Church traveled
the same route that the Scottish Church had taken in a much
shorter time. So completely did the new ideas take the field that
until recently neither Scottish Presbyterian nor Dutch Reformed
would ever imagine that his was by tradition a fully liturgical
church.

The story in Reformed Germany can be told more briefly because it followed the same course as that in the Netherlands and
indeed under Dutch influence. The resistance was greater in Germany, possibly because of an innate conservatism or because the
Lutheran influence was much more strongly felt.

History reveals the same synodical protests against pietism as
in the Netherlands. In 1677 (seven years after Labadie's arrival
in Germany) the Synod of Cleves took an action which was later
endorsed by the General Synod.

> For the better edification and comfort of the ignorant the
> customary formularies shall on ordinary occasions in connection
> with the preaching be adhered to; still freedom shall be allowed,
> at special times and occasions, to add some things to the ordi-
> nary prayers or even to form other prayers, agreeing with the
> Scriptures and the matter of the forms prescribed—provided
> (and this was added by the General Synod) that the customary
> formularies should not thereby by contemptuously set aside.[12]

We can see German pietism at work in one of the pietist historian's description of the reforms made in St. Martin's Church in
Bremen by Theodore Untereyck, a leader in the movement, who
became its minister in 1670. Listing the customs which Untereyck
sought to destroy (he was not wholly successful), his biographer
says:

> Bremen was a large and wealthy, but gay and worldly city. . . .
> As it was surrounded on every side by Lutheran cities, it, al-
> though Reformed, still retained some Lutheran customs. Thus
> after the Lutheran fashion, the Reformed ministers preached on

the pericopes . . . gave private communion, the congregation used hymns as well as psalms, celebrated the Lord's Supper every Sunday.[13]

The list of Lutheranisms is amusing. No one did more than the pietists themselves to introduce hymns into the worship of the Reformed Church. And surely John Calvin would have been surprised to learn that a weekly celebration of the Lord's Supper was a Lutheranism! But the list is interesting not only for what it reveals about the worship of a German Reformed congregation in the seventeenth century but for what it reveals about the liturgical items to which the pietists objected.

That the movement was not so successful in its sweep in Germany as it had been in the Netherlands is indicated by the fact that in 1728 (a few years before Ravestein declared that no respectable Dutch minister used the liturgy any longer) the General Synod in Germany was still legislating.

> Since it does not become any individual minister, yea, not even a provincial Synod to make any changes in the administration of the Word of God, the Holy Supper, Holy Baptism, and the form of conducting worship, as handed down to us; but such changes must be undertaken, after mature consideration . . . by the reverend General Synod.[14]

There is a still more striking evidence of the liturgical persistence of the German churches. It is a hymnal, an American edition of which was published by Christopher Saur in Germantown, Pennsylvania, in 1763. The title page of the American edition informs us that this book was used in the "Reformed churches in Hesse, Hanover, the Palatinate, and Pennsylvania." In addition to the psalms and hymns, the book contains the liturgical collects, epistles, and gospels for every Sunday as well as for all the festival and saints' days. There is also a collection of prayers and the Heidelberg Catechism. Such a book is interesting not only for its indication of the long persistence of liturgical life in the German churches, but also for its indication of the early habits of worship of one of the churches in our own country.

But even though the movement developed more slowly in Germany, the final result was about the same as in the Netherlands.

Max Göbel, a historian of the Reformed churches in Germany, says that once pietism had been permitted to make adaptations in the liturgy "the custom and caprice of free prayer began to prevail to such an extent" that during the eighteenth century the liturgy was gradually "altogether dislodged."[15] In 1817 the majority of the Reformed churches in Germany united with most of the Lutheran churches. The liturgical story of the united church, beginning with the Prussian Agenda, is more properly a Lutheran story.

In France and in the French-speaking cantons of Switzerland we become aware of another influence on the liturgy. For most of the time under discussion, these churches showed complete liturgical integrity. It was not until the nineteenth century that they experienced anything like pietism—and then under the auspices of Scottish evangelicalism.

If there was any outside influence on the French Church during the seventeenth century it was Anglicanism, with which there were many close contacts. It is striking to find many of the theologians of the French Church during this time in favor of some form of episcopacy. As the English Puritans took refuge in the Netherlands, the royalist and Anglican refugees tended, during Cromwell's time, to flee to France. John Cosin, later Bishop of Durham, was a regular worshiper at the Reformed Church in Charenton during his exile.

It is also possible that in so royalist a country as France a tolerated minority like the Reformed Church was well advised to take its model from England rather than from republics like Holland or Switzerland. In any event, when the Huguenot congregations in colonial America gave up their separate existence, most of them entered neither the Presbyterian nor the Dutch Reformed churches (there were, of course, exceptions) but became Anglican. While this contact with Anglicanism, accompanied by a strong distrust of Puritanism, made no immediate changes liturgically, it doubtless tended to a maintenance of the full liturgy in the French Church.

The revocation of the Edict of Nantes in 1685 brought the official life of the French Church to an end. From 1685 to 1787 it

lived underground or, as the French say, "in the desert." In such
a situation, when services were held in the open air and often dismissed at a moment's notice, it might be expected that the liturgy
would have been sacrificed as a non-essential. That expectation
would seem all the more justified when we recall that one of the
products of this century in the desert was the rise of Huguenot
prophetism. J. D. Benoit describes it for us.

> The "prophets of the Cévennes," as they are called, were
> preachers who would fall into a state of trance and pronounce
> impassioned discourses. . . . Women, girls, and even children,
> falling under the influence of inspiration, became prophets and
> prophetesses. There were visions, sometimes accompanied by
> convulsive movements, and inflammatory invective directed
> against "great Babylon" (the Roman Church).[16]

Such experiences certainly entered deeply into Huguenot piety
and worship. The century of persecution engendered in the
French Reformed mind a deep distaste for any of the symbols of
Roman Catholicism, altars, crosses, or crucifixes. But even so, it is
amazing to what extent even in the desert the French Church
preserved its liturgical life. As early as 1716 one of the desert
synods voted:

> We shall observe the same form in the public acts of worship
> that we observed in the time of freedom and that is still observed
> in the churches of Geneva and Switzerland.[17]

Decisions of that sort were renewed several times as the century
continued. Despite the popularity of prophetism, the leaders of
the desert church, men such as Antoine Court (who founded a
seminary in Lausanne to train a ministry for France) and later
Paul Rabaut, were determined that the church should not lose its
liturgical identity.

Family prayer books for the use of Reformed families were
published in Holland or Switzerland during this time and smug-
gled into France. One such collection, published in Amsterdam in
1758, contained all the liturgical prayers and forms together with
other devotional materials. One of the rubrics in this volume is of
interest. In addition to the liturgical materials a few sermons had
been included, with this directive.

The head of the family, after this prayer, will read the text
which has been chosen and the sermon, reading with special
application, pausing at the end of each sentence, trying to imitate the pronunciation of a preacher.[18]

But while the persecuted French Church was thus trying to
maintain its integrity strange things were happening in Geneva.
The beginning of the eighteenth century saw an increasing relaxa-
tion of theological orthodoxy in that city, a movement which continued until the Genevan Church reached the Socinianism sati-
rized by Voltaire.

The first great prophet of this movement was Jean Alphonse
Turretin, the last of a distinguished family of Italian refugees
who had played a significant part in the theological history of
Geneva. Partly educated in England, Turretin was much impressed by Anglicanism and especially the Latitudinarian party.
Returning to Geneva, he became professor of church history in
1697, resolved to liberalize the reigning theology in his native
city. A man of persuasive charm and great ability, he was largely
successful in a city which had grown weary of the sterile literalism
and scholastic quodlibetarianism of orthodoxy.

This movement to rationalism, as it came to be called, was in-
spired by precisely the same thing as the movement to pietism—
the failure and futility of orthodoxy. But the liberal movement
had a different liturgical result from the pietist movement. A man
like Turretin was not anti-liturgical. His Anglican sympathies
alone would have prevented that. But there was a certain decency
and order about the liturgy that appealed to all the rationalist
school. Ostensibly they were all friends of the liturgy. Their ob-
jection, shared by Turretin, was that the liturgy failed to reflect
the new theology. Not only its language but also its ideology was
antiquated.[19]

In 1724 Turretin was authorized to produce a revision of the
liturgy in Geneva. Another revision followed in 1743, a few years
after his death. The one spot that Calvin had left for free prayer,
the prayer before the sermon, was removed in this revision and a
liturgical prayer substituted. There was to be no chance for the
entry of any pious enthusiasm in the worship of the church in

Geneva. Other enrichments included the addition of a service of confirmation (a reflection of Turretin's stay in England) as well as a lectionary and table of hymns for special occasions.

Actually the structural changes were not great. Following the example of morning prayer as he had known it in England, Turretin tried to persuade the Genevan authorities to relocate the great prayer of thanksgiving and intercession before rather than after the sermon, but they refused.[20] The real revisions came not in structure but in language. Closely as the liturgy resembled Calvin's in structure, the language introduced an entirely new theology.

Several illustrations can be made.[21] Calvin's confession had read,

> We are poor sinners, conceived and born in iniquity and corruption, inclined to do evil, useless for any good.

The Genevan revision improved our condition somewhat, although the form finally adopted was not so optimistic as Turretin had wished.

> We are poor sinners, born in corruption, inclined to evil, incapable of doing good by ourselves.

The changes in the sacramental forms were even more striking. "Regeneration" in the baptismal liturgy was replaced with an elaborate periphrasis, "a very great change in us and a renunciation of everything in our nature that is impure and vicious." "The blood of Jesus Christ will cleanse us from all sin" now read "in communion with our Savior we find everything necessary to purify our souls."

The typical language of the enlightenment, however, is best seen in the phrase from the liturgy for the Eucharist:

> We do not consider the Holy Supper as an empty and ineffectual ceremony, but remember that it contains everything that is most sacred and consoling in religion.

Compare that with Calvin's language at the same point and it is obvious how far we have come.

These liturgical revisions were in the interest of the new theology of the enlightenment. No longer a sinner in need of redemption man was now an unfortunate creature in need of help and instruction. The gospel and sacraments had become the offices of religion, designed for our education and consolation. Incarnation and atonement had both largely disappeared in favor of teaching and example. It is not difficult to understand some of the eighteenth-century pietist invective against the liturgy when we see the theological direction in which the liturgy was moving.

In the end the rationalist liberalization of the liturgy led to its destruction just as surely as the pietist disuse of it. For not everyone in Switzerland shared in this theological latitudinarianism. Some liturgical provision had to be made for the orthodox. The result in many Swiss churches was a double liturgy, one for the liberals and the other for conservatives. Sometimes it was done with considerable ingenuity. Prayers would begin with identical phrases and then move in totally different directions.

But usually there were simply two of everything. A prayer containing all the traditional language of the theology of the Reformation was followed by an alternate from which almost every trace of Christian influence had been removed. The custom of providing a book of varied liturgical possibilities, so popular today (a modern critic has likened such books to the menu in a restaurant), was first introduced to satisfy every possible theological point of view. But once that had happened there was really no liturgy at all, because there was no longer any work of the people, any voice of the church.

To conclude this chapter we shall pay an imaginary visit to a Reformed service in the eighteenth century. It would be much the same whether we chose Scotland, Switzerland, Germany, or the Netherlands. The order of service would be much the same whether or not the congregation used the liturgy.

In most cases it would be a preaching service. Though for very different reasons, both pietism and rationalism discouraged frequent celebrations of the Eucharist. Infrequent communions were the rule in pietism because of the awesomeness of the occasion; in rationalism because of the embarrassment of irrationality. But the result was the same. Annual celebrations or even more infrequent ones were not uncommon. In pietist circles only a small fraction of the congregation shared in these services, the spiritually elite who did not fear to eat and drink damnation to themselves. Calvin's vision of Word and Sacrament was completely lost by either party as the pulpit came to obscure the Table.

In almost all situations the service would have begun with the so-called reader's service. This custom had come into being as a substitute for the organ prelude at a time when organs were not permitted. As the congregation was gathering, a layman read chapters from the Bible. It had the advantage also of maintaining a kind of witness to the place of the layman in worship. In fact, in some countries (the custom still continues in one of the Dutch Reformed churches in South Africa) the reader's duties were extended so that he took the opening part of the service down to the first psalm. During the singing of this psalm the minister made his entrance, sometimes pausing to bow to the distinguished members of his congregation.

The singing must have been uniformly bad. Liturgical writers from almost every country all complain about it. Here, for example, is Maxwell's comment about music in the Church of Scotland during this period.

> During this period also . . . metrical psalmody grievously declined. . . . The revival was, however, long-delayed; for it was stultified for nearly two hundred years by the introduction at this time from England of the revolting practice of "lining," which, while it endured, made any real recovery impossible. "Lining" was the practice of the precentor reading, or singing in a monotone or according to some private method of his own, one line of a metrical psalm, after which the people sang that line as near to the tune specified as they could get (and this was often not recognizably near it). . . . Its deplorable effect upon congregational singing surpasses the power of the mind to imagine.[22]

Apparently the practice of "lining" was peculiar to the British Isles. But the fact that it was not used in Reformed churches on the continent did not seem to make for better music. Here is what Doumergue has to say about the singing in the French Church:

The precentor was one of the creations of Huguenot piety, sometimes very disagreeable, sometimes very picturesque. Unfortunately one remembers more of the ways in which he irritated than of the ways in which he charmed . . . with his old psalmbook held in both hands to beat time. . . .

The Huguenot precentor sang vociferously sometimes, but usually without taking any great notice of the music or of its directions. I can still hear a precentor whom I knew . . . and it was only rarely that the notes which he sang bore any relation to the notes on the page.[23]

Similar testimony could be added from Holland. There were no choirs at this time in Reformed churches. For the most part only the psalms were sung in worship, although strong pietist influence had added some hymns in some places. It was toward the end of the eighteenth century that the metrical paraphrases, versifications of other parts of Scripture besides the Psalter, came into use in Scotland.

In almost all of the continental churches, though not in Britain, the Ten Commandments would have been read at the beginning of the service, sometimes by the reader, sometimes by the minister. Where a liturgical confession of sin was not used, the prayer which preceded the sermon usually contained one.

Directly after this prayer came the reading and preaching of the Word. In Scotland the reading was often accompanied by a lengthy verse-by-verse explanation which amounted to another sermon. It was a practice against which successive General Assemblies protested, but largely in vain. It reflected the English Puritan horror of what was called "dumb reading," a dangerous relict of popery. Though it never seems to have been taken up to any great extent in the continental Reformed churches, its roots actually go back to Bucer who had required a similar practice for whichever of the two lessons in the liturgy was not to be used as the text for the sermon. It is, therefore, only an extreme example of that didacticism of which Reformed worship has always been fond, a refusal to do anything without accompanying it with a full and adequate explanation.

The great prayer still followed the sermon whether or not the liturgical form was used. If it was not, the service concluded with a long prayer of mixed content and often of prodigious length. For some divines a prayer lasting half an hour was only a warm-up! Our custom of placing it earlier in the service (the very thing which Turretin had wished in Geneva) did not begin until the nineteenth century and then under the same influence of Anglican morning prayer.

It would be misleading to give the impression that in those churches which did not use the liturgical prayers there was no real praying. On the contrary, some of these free prayers which were written down and have been preserved indicate a high liturgical sense even though cast in a nonliturgical form. But many others were monstrous perversions of corporate prayer, mere private meditations and exhortations carried on in public. In liturgical churches the great prayer was always concluded with the Lord's Prayer, though the congregation merely listened and did not join in saying it. In pietist and Puritan circles the Lord's Prayer was never used.

During this period the Apostles' Creed (the Nicene had never been used in Reformed churches) fell into general disuse except at the infrequent celebrations of the Eucharist. The Dutch and German liturgies did make use of it at the afternoon or evening service. Again it was a form with which neither pietist nor Puritan would have anything to do.

The absence of the offertory from the services of this period is to be explained by the fact that the offerings were always received at the door as the worshiper entered or left the church. In most of the Reformed churches it would have been an offering only for the poor since the church itself was supported by the state.

One final remark must be made to indicate that the service in this time was conducted entirely from the pulpit. Indeed, there was probably no table in the church. It was brought in when needed and that usually was very seldom. But as the only piece of furniture in many churches, the pulpit was usually a very handsome thing indeed, always of commanding height, usually elaborately carved, often surmounted by an equally ornate canopy or sounding board. It bore little relationship to the small desk on a low platform with which we have become so familiar. In Holland, where objections to organs disappeared very early in the Reformed Church, the organ case was often equally ornate.

At the beginning of the nineteenth century the situation of Reformed Church worship could be described in this way. In some places the historic liturgy had been preserved as a museum piece. In others it had been altered into an expression of something like least common denominator religion. Always didactic in tone, Reformed liturgies easily lent themselves to recasting as theological summaries, whatever the theology to be summarized. France and French Switzerland were the chief illustrations of this situation, though there were a few others. As late as 1820 the Synod of the French churches in the Bernese Jura ordered its ministers to follow the liturgy "exactly, literally, without adding or subtracting a single word."[24]

In Great Britain, the Netherlands, much of Germany, and the United States, the liturgy had almost entirely disappeared. A few sacramental forms and the skeletal remains of an order of service survived in some churches to witness to the fact, increasingly incredible with the passing of time, that the Reformed churches had once had a liturgical life. Kneeling or standing for prayer and standing for praise, once good Reformed customs, had been replaced by sitting for everything. The Christian year had almost entirely disappeared. The Eucharist was so infrequent as to be negligible. The one significant element in a service, symbolized by the one imposing piece of furniture in the church, was the sermon.

In many ways pietism, which was largely responsible for this liturgical situation, had been a necessary and even a helpful reaction. But it lacked any real doctrine of the church. Indeed, its individualism basically contradicted any real doctrine of the church. Because of that basic flaw, if the pietist did not actively oppose the liturgy, especially when it became identified with liberalism, he simply ignored it as unnecessary folderol. (One is tempted to add that his situation has not changed.) To that extent pietism must bear a full share of responsibility for the situation we have described.

The impartial observer surveying the liturgical life of the Reformed churches in, let us say, 1820 could have justifiably concluded that it was just about finished. But at that very moment those same churches were at the beginning of a liturgical development that was to prove more productive than any in their history.

III

THE GOTHIC AGE

Because we divide history into centuries, it is an easy thing for us to divide the history of any movement into these same centuries. Thus we can easily assume that the end of the eighteenth century marked the end of the decline of worship in the Reformed churches and that the beginning of the nineteenth century marked the beginning of recovery. That would not be true. In some places the decline continued at the same time the recovery was beginning in others. There are places in which the decline continues in our own time.

The same habit of thinking could lead us to assume that during the seventeenth and eighteenth centuries there were no signs of recovery anywhere. And that would not be true either. For in the early years of the eighteenth century there was in one of the Reformed churches a liturgical reform of literally astounding proportions. At the time, it had little influence beyond its own small area. But more than a century later it had come to be considered one of the great landmarks on the way of liturgical recovery. Though not entirely free from both the rationalism and pietism which so nearly wrecked the liturgy in these centuries, it stands as a kind of lonely harbinger of things to come in an age of liturgical sterility.

The liturgy in question was the Liturgy of the Churches of Neuchâtel and Vallangin, two small places in Switzerland. First published in 1713, it was the work of Jean Frederic Ostervald, "a

churchman in the grand manner" as Karl Barth once called him.[1]
At this point a small correction should be made. In one way the
influence of this liturgy reached far beyond its own small territory, for it became the official liturgy of the Huguenot congregation in Charleston, South Carolina, the last survivor of the original Huguenot churches in this country. In 1853 the Charleston
church had it published in English.[2] Ostervald's liturgy, therefore,
can qualify as one of the liturgies actually used in both colonial
and modern America. And, as we shall see, the English translation
played a part in the liturgical recovery in nineteenth-century
Scotland.

Something must be said about Jean Frederic Ostervald since
this liturgy is entirely his work. Born in the town of Neuchâtel in
1663, his education was similar to that of Turretin's in Geneva
who was his close friend. In view of the large influence of
Anglicanism on his liturgy, it is strange that Ostervald never
visited England. His basic training was received at that celebrated Academy in Saumur, France, which the orthodox were
beginning to suspect because of the theology taught there by the
liberal Moses Amyraut. Ordained to the ministry in Neuchâtel in
1683, Ostervald never again left his native city. He died there in
1747, having served for some years as dean of the town.

Though he never visited England, Ostervald was well known
there. In 1700 he was elected a member of the Society for the
Propagation of the Gospel. He became the friend and correspond-
ent of such Anglican leaders as Archbishop William Wake and
Bishop Gilbert Burnet. As dean of Neuchâtel, he probably considered himself a bishop. In his correspondence with his Anglican
friends there was even discussion of possible schemes of reunion.
But that is another story.

This Anglican correspondence, carried on with some of the
leaders of the Latitudinarian party, gave Ostervald an increasing
admiration for the Anglican position as he understood it. His mind
had already been predisposed toward theological liberalism by
his education at Saumur and his private study with Claude Pajon,
one of the liberal leaders in the French Church. But now his study
of Anglicanism was to give him a new perspective on the liturgy.

His dissatisfaction with the Neuchâtel liturgy was first expressed in 1701. That liturgy did not follow the Calvinist pattern but was a modified form of Farel's *Manner and Fashion* and so was of Zwinglian cast. Writing to his friend Turretin in Geneva he said,

> It is supremely important to think of the reformation of worship, for it is in a deplorable way among us. Our opponents are right when they say that Calvin introduced a form of worship unknown to antiquity.[3]

During the ensuing year Ostervald had been giving thought to the question and had even made some preliminary study. In 1702 he wrote:

> Our plan is to draw up what can be called *Divine Service*. It cannot be said that we have it now. Under the pretext of reformation our reformers have horribly disfigured it. We want to restore to our worship all of the essential features: adoration, praise, the confession of sin, reading, and prayers.[4]

It must have been about this time that Ostervald set to work on a new liturgy. By 1706 he had the manuscript of it ready and submitted it to several friends. But its publication and introduction in Neuchâtel were delayed till 1713, and even then it met bitter opposition. That it was ready long before its formal introduction is evidenced by the fact that an English translation of it, made for the benefit of his Anglican friends, was published in Basel in 1712, a year before the official French version in Neuchâtel.[5]

The preface is almost of greater interest than the liturgy itself. It could be called the first liturgical manifesto in the Reformed churches. Here are some of Ostervald's more significant sentences:

> When the order of divine service is settled, it is celebrated as well by the Minister as by the People, in a manner more edifying, grave, and decorous than when it is entrusted to the discretion of the Clergy. The preservation of uniformity in worship is another valuable consequence of Liturgies. . . .
>
> In matters of worship, the practice of the past ages of the Church is entitled to great consideration. . . .
>
> In truth, the people ought not to attend on divine service merely as auditors and spectators, nor ought they merely to fol-

low in thought that which is uttered by the ministers of the
church; but they ought also to speak on their part, and at least
to answer Amen to all that is spoken in the name of the assembly. It is admitted that the ancient mode of celebrating service
was by parts or intervals, and by antiphones, that is to say, responses. . . . The primitive Christians retained this practice in
their worship, and especially in that excellent and admirable
Liturgy which they employed for the communion service. . . .
   But one of the principal objects contemplated in the form of
worship for the ordinary Morning and Evening service, was to
re-establish the reading of the Scriptures, as a part of public
worship. . . .
   The sermons were at first only an interruption of worship and
an addition to the reading, and were not regarded, as by many
at the present day, the most important part of public service,
and the principal object for which the people assembled. . . .
Nor does it suffice that they be read in the churches before the
assembly is formed, or the worship commences. Such reading
does not constitute a part of divine service.[6]

Ostervald's Sunday service follows the traditional structure of
the Calvinist pattern, with many modifications borrowed from the
Book of Common Prayer. The use of the Ten Commandments and
the form for the confession of sin are Calvin's. But the use of the
Lord's Prayer after the confession of sin rather than at the end of
the service is an Anglicanism, one which, incidentally, is still
found in most Reformed and Presbyterian churches in which the
Lord's Prayer follows the "Invocation." The influence of Anglican
Morning Prayer is to be seen in the use of two lessons from a
fixed lectionary, the use of canticles, the use of the Creed after
the second lesson, and the placing of all the prayers of thanksgiving and intercession before the sermon, something which
Turretin had unsuccessfully tried to do in Geneva.
   Ostervald's new liturgy also included forms for daily morning
and evening prayer without a sermon. He had compiled a very
extensive treasury of prayers not only for the festivals of the
Christian year but for special occasions and needs. While some of
these were his own composition, the majority were borrowed from
the liturgies of other churches.
   The Eucharistic liturgy is contained in a separate sacramental

section. It represents the most complete break with previous tradition. Large parts of Calvin's Eucharistic form were used in the
old Neuchâtel liturgy, despite its Zwinglian structure. These
found no favor in Ostervald's eyes.

> I believe that you will agree that the liturgy of the Holy Sup-
> per in use among us is no good at all. Indeed, it can hardly be
> called a liturgy. It has absolutely nothing in common with the
> way in which the eucharist was celebrated in the primitive
> church. It is a dry harangue, without any unction, into which
> Calvin has inserted his ideas about partaking of the substance of
> the flesh and blood of Jesus Christ, ideas as absurd as those of
> the papists.[7]

So significant a liturgical reform as Ostervald's is deserving of
evaluation. At first sight it had much to commend it. It is the first
real prayer book in the Reformed churches, providing not only
the invariable structure and materials for worship but a full set of
necessary variables for the Christian year. That dull monotony
which had been such a feature of Reformed Church worship has
completely disappeared in Ostervald's revision.

Ostervald must also be commended for his recognition that in
the liturgy the devotional is more important than the didactic.
Convinced as they were of the close connection between creed
and cultus, the early Reformed liturgists had provided far too
much explanatory material and far too little that was material
for worship. By Ostervald's time even that little had largely disappeared, till Reformed liturgies tended to be hardly more than
didactic statements, "dry harangues," as he aptly called them. It
was his genius that he understood that this is not the true character of liturgy, that the people of God must be provided with
aids to worship, not with theological expositions.

His insistence on the necessity for corporate participation in
worship also has a welcome sound. In an age in which worship
had become a ministerial monologue, save for the singing of
psalms, Ostervald did not hesitate to assert the true Reformed
principle of worship as a corporate act. He would have been
surprised to discover what a good Calvinist he was in this insistence. But where Calvin had used singing as the response of

the congregation, Ostervald, following Anglican custom, employed the said response.

Finally, it is in Ostervald that we hear, at least for the first time since the Reformation, the ecumenical note, expressed in his desire to bring worship into conformity with the practice of the church in all ages. It will be more than a century before it is sounded again in the Reformed churches. To evidence his ecumenical intention Ostervald did not hesitate to reintroduce into his liturgy material from traditional Christian liturgy which had been banned from Reformed Church worship since the Reformation: the Sursum Corda, the Sanctus, the Gloria in Excelsis.

But all of these attractive features must not blind us to the essential weaknesses of Ostervald's reform. For in the final sense, it just missed greatness. Jean Frederic Ostervald was, after all, a child of his time, a man of the eighteenth century. That position made it impossible for him to understand the real thrust of the Calvinistic Reformation. Nor did his emotional reaction against the dry and scholastic Calvinism which he knew, the dessicated liturgical forms with which he was familiar, help.

This limitation comes out in Ostervald's slighting reference to preaching as an "interruption," fully indicative of the way in which the Reformed mind of the eighteenth century had totally lost the Reformation concept of the Word as a means of grace. It comes out even more strongly in his tart observation about Calvin's theories of the Eucharistic presence. How ironic that it should be Calvin, the despised didactic, who was the true Catholic here while Ostervald, for all his Anglicanism, remained an eighteenth-century sectarian.

But the most striking liturgical failure is to be found in Ostervald's lack of awareness of Calvin's insistence on the liturgical unity of Word and Sacrament. Here again Calvin was much more ecumenical and primitive than Ostervald, for all his ecumenical borrowings. In spite of all its catholic enrichments, Ostervald's Eucharist is much more foreign to the shape of the *liturgy* than the despised and didactic liturgy of John Calvin. If only he could have used Calvin's catholic liturgical structure and Calvin's Eucharistic theology as the basis for his enrichments and im-

provements, Ostervald might have changed the whole history of
the worship of the Reformed churches. But the time was not
ready. With all of its valuable insights and enriching additions,
Ostervald's liturgy has the stamp of the enlightenment of the
eighteenth century upon it.

The rise and fall of Napoleon is often taken as the end of the
age of enlightenment and the beginning of the romantic era.
Whether that be accurate, it is at least convenient. And there is
something to be said for such a dating. For certainly the cata-
clysm of the French Revolution and the succeeding European
holocaust shook the prevailing faith in the rationality and nobil-
ity of human nature in much the same way that the First World
War shook the foundations of theological liberalism.

For whatever reason, in the closing years of the eighteenth
century and the opening years of the nineteenth the center of
interest shifted from Greek and Roman antiquity to the Middle
Ages, from Classic to Gothic. The change can be seen in architecture; it can be seen in literature; inevitably it had to be seen in
liturgy. The Oxford Movement in the Church of England and
the so-called High Church Movement in German Lutheranism
are two illustrations. Sooner or later the change had to involve the
Reformed churches as well.

But in the case of the Reformed churches it would obviously be
later. Much more than the Anglican or Lutheran churches, the
Reformed churches had reacted against the Middle Ages. It is not
surprising, therefore, to find that in the early years of the Gothic
age most of the Reformed authors were rather patronizing in their
sneers about "Puseyism, Medieval monkery," and that sort of
thing. So completely had any liturgical consciousness lapsed in
most Reformed circles that the Anglican and Lutheran liturgical
revivals were often greeted derisively while the liturgical chaos of
the Reformed churches was often held up to praise as a model of
apostolic simplicity. Let others, less fortunate and enlightened,
play with the mumbo-jumbo of medievalism; it shall not come
nigh us!

But even the Reformed churches live in the world. The fever
of the Gothic age eventually began to infect them too. The first

indication was architectural as Reformed meetinghouses began to affect spires, pointed windows, or galleries hung between Gothic arches. Doubtless Gothic romanticism began to influence the secret aspiration of individual members of the Reformed churches before it was felt in the official life of those communions. In 1861, when in some places a Reformed liturgical revival was already under way, the Genevan philosopher, Henri Amiel, confided to his Journal.

> Our churches are too little open; our churchyards too much. The result in both cases is the same. The tortured and trembling heart which seeks, outside the scene of its daily miseries, to find some place where it may pray in peace, or pour out its grief before God, or meditate in the presence of eternal things, with us has nowhere to go. Our Church ignores these wants of the soul instead of divining and meeting them. She shows very little compassionate care for her children, very little wise consideration for the more delicate griefs, and no intuition of the deeper mysteries of tenderness, no religious suavity. Under a pretext of spirituality we are always checking legitimate aspirations. We have lost the mystical sense; and what is religion without mysticism?[8]

Amiel's is the complaint of the romantic against the liturgical coldness of the Reformed churches. How many others felt as he did it is impossible to say. But judging from the ready response which the liturgical revival met in the Reformed churches when it came, there must have been a considerable number.

When it came, it happened everywhere at about the same time. The impulse toward liturgical improvement seems almost simultaneously to have taken hold of men in Reformed churches as widely scattered as those of Scotland, France, Switzerland, and the United States of America. The only major Reformed church to be unaffected by this nineteenth-century revival was that of the Netherlands.

It would be striking to claim that this revival began in the United States and that thus, for once, there was a movement that went from here to Europe. That would be an exaggerated claim. But it can be said that liturgical stirrings began to be felt here as early as anywhere and that in some ways they did influence the same developments in Britain and Europe.

The earliest reference to the subject I have been able to find is in an address delivered in Philadelphia in 1835 by one of the most colorful pulpit celebrities of the day, Dr. George Washington Bethune. "A great pigface of a man," as Templeton Strong described him, Dr. Bethune, the son of a wealthy New York merchant, had graduated from Princeton Seminary in 1826. But he finally chose to enter the ministry of the Dutch Reformed Church. This was one of the reasons which he gave:

> The Reformed Dutch Church has a liturgy adapted to all the offices and occasions of worship . . . it is perhaps to be regretted that its disuse . . . has become so general among us, from perhaps a weak desire to conform to the habits of other denominations. Certainly there are occasions when the forms of prayer are at least as edifying as many extemporaneous effusions we hear from the desk and it is evident that the wise fathers of the Church did not intend that they should remain a dead letter in our books.[9]

The tentativeness of the observation shows that Bethune felt that he was breaking new ground. But he was typical of the awakening consciousness of many Reformed and Presbyterian ministers. Especially in the New York area (though the same thing was happening at the same time in Scotland) there were at this time many secessions to the Episcopal Church. The slovenly and careless worship of the Reformed churches was often cited as a principal reason for the change, though social reasons doubtless played a very large role. But men like Dr. Bethune, troubled by the leakage, were anxious to plug this hole in the dyke if they could.

The revision and improvement of the Dutch Reformed Church became one of his chief ambitions. He finally achieved it in 1857 with the first official revision of the liturgy of any of the Dutch churches since 1619. It was a very mild revision. But it did provide a complete Sunday service instead of the two prayers to which the Sunday liturgy had dwindled, a new marriage service, and a lectionary. What was most surprising, it contained an office for the burial of the dead. Up to this time, no Reformed liturgy had ever dared try such a daring experiment, flirting as it did with all the dangers of popery.

While Dr. Bethune was spurring the Dutch Reformed Church to a consideration of its liturgy, there began to be similar stirrings in the German Reformed Church (today part of the United Church of Christ). Much more familiar with developments in Europe than its Dutch cousin, some of the German church leaders were aware of the liturgical movement in the recently formed United Evangelical Church in Prussia.

An even more powerful influence, however, was the *Reformirtes Kirchenbuch* which had been published in Zurich in 1847 by J. H. A. Ebrard, one of the theological faculty there. Ebrard's book was a pioneer work, a thesaurus of prayers, services, and offices, all taken from continental Reformed liturgies, arranged for the Christian year and supplemented with materials from the Anglican Prayer Book and Ebrard's own pen. In some of the German-speaking congregations of Pennsylvania it was actually used in place of the old liturgy of the sixteenth century or of a rather clumsy revision which had been made to succeed it.

A combination of influences from Europe and dissatisfaction with their liturgy led in 1848 to the appointment of a committee to draft a new liturgy for the German Reformed Church. That committee did not produce its provisional report until 1857 or its final work till 1866. That final report and the material which accompanied it were of such a nature as to require extended consideration later. At the time we are discussing, various preliminary materials and studies of this German Reformed committee were available in published form.

These activities were bound to produce an effect in American Presbyterianism, especially since it seems to have been the heaviest loser to the Episcopal Church. In 1853 a curious volume was published entitled "A Presbyterian Minister looking for the Church—by one of Three Hundred." It was a long-winded and petulant attack on the Presbyterian Church by a former minister who had become an Episcopal clergyman and therefore chose to remain anonymous. Objections to Presbyterian worship figured largely in its pages, some of them rather shrewd hits. It does not seem possible that the title meant that three hundred Presbyterian ministers had become Episcopalians. But it could well have meant that in the author's opinion that number were unhappy and enviously eyeing the Anglican pasture. Even in Princeton Seminary, that bulwark of Presbyterian conservatism, Dr. James Alexander had ventured some suggestions for liturgical improvements.

The Presbyterian pioneer, however, was Dr. Charles Washington Baird, the son of a close friend of Dr. Bethune. Graduating from Union Seminary in 1852, Baird served as minister of the American Church in Rome for two years and then returned to this country to become secretary of the American and Foreign Church Union.

In 1855 Baird published *Eutaxia* or *The Presbyterian Liturgies*. Though it may have come as a shock to some Presbyterians, *Eutaxia* contained nothing new or startling. For the most part it was a description of the liturgies of Calvin and Knox, with some specimen forms. Baird claimed that Calvin's liturgy had been a significant influence in the framing of the English *Book of Common Prayer*. That claim is open to a good deal of question, but at the time it probably gave those renegade Presbyterians in the Episcopal Church something to think about. That was probably Baird's intention. He also made some flattering references to the liturgy of the Reformed Dutch Church as the only surviving example of what had once been the universal usage of the Reformed churches.

In 1857, encouraged by the reception of *Eutaxia*, Baird published a second volume, *A Book of Public Prayer*. Somewhat resembling Ebrard's collection, this was a compilation of prayers and services from all the early liturgies of such men as Calvin, Bucer, and Knox. Perhaps the author felt that such a collection might come to be used as a kind of prayer book in the pews of Presbyterian churches, or at least in their pulpits.

If that was his intention, he was a little late, for in 1856 there had appeared in New York a similar volume:

> Preces Ecclesiasticae: the Forms of Public Devotion, instituted by Calvin, John Knox, Martin Bucer, Micronius, and other Pres-

byterian Divines; adopted and used in various branches of the Presbyterian Church.

The compiler chose to remain anonymous, but he had obviously read *Eutaxia* and then rushed into print himself. The next decade, in fact, saw the publication of many such service books under Presbyterian and Reformed auspices. At last Reformed churchmen could hold up their liturgical heads! They too had a tradition, prayer books, and liturgies, every bit as ancient, though somewhat less thoroughly used, as those of their Anglican neighbors.

The scene must now be shifted to Britain, where in 1856 Baird's *Eutaxia* enjoyed an English edition. Its sponsor, who added both a preface and introduction, was Dr. Thomas Binney, a Congregationalist, minister of the historic King's Weigh House in London (the same church which in another century was the scene of Dr. Orchard's "Free Catholic" experiments). We can easily assume that Baird's book soon found its way to Glasgow and Edinburgh. And a timely arrival it was, since events at that time in Scotland seemed to indicate that there were liturgical stirrings in the Kirk.

In 1857 Dr. Robert Lee, minister of Old Greyfriars' in Edinburgh had begun those liturgical reforms which would attract the attention of the entire Scottish Church. Old Greyfriars had been reopened for worship in that year. Not only did Dr. Lee ask the people to kneel for prayer and stand for praise as they worshiped in their renovated sanctuary, he actually read the prayers in the service from his own book, *Prayers for Public Worship*, which had been published that same year.

Here is how it appeared to a somewhat hostile critic.

An experiment has been lately tried in Edinburgh respecting the method of celebrating public worship, which, if not interfered with by the Church judicatories . . . may lead to important consequences. Dr. Robert Lee, on the reopening of Old Greyfriars' Church, is said to have deviated to a somewhat startling extent from the accustomed manner among us of conducting the public worship of God in the sanctuary. Very plain and ungainly the ancient building of Old Greyfriars was. . . But on entering, a somewhat novel spectable is presented. With more or less taste, every window has been filled with stained glass, to an extent, we confess, that suggests the idea almost of a religious toy. . . .

Nor is this the whole amount of the alteration, if rumor be correct. . . . The clergyman is said to read the prayers out of a book, and the people are alleged to be invited at the close of each branch of the petitions to give their response, thus audibly expressing their concurrence with what has been uttered.[10]

Dr. Lee's prayers were not drawn from any collection of ancient models. They were his own composition and to a large degree reflected his latitudinarian theology. He had no interest in or knowledge of the liturgies of antiquity or of the Reformation. A kind of Scottish Ostervald, he was distressed by the condition of public worship and proposed to do something about it. In 1863 he added a harmonium to the furnishings of Old Greyfriars', replacing it with a pipe organ in 1865.

These goings-on had to come to the attention of the ecclesiastical authorities. In 1859 the General Assembly, avoiding discussion of many of Dr. Lee's improvements, did pronounce on his reading of prayers.

Find that this practice is an innovation upon and contrary to the laws and usage of the Church, . . . and the Assembly enjoin Dr. Lee to discontinue the use of the book in question in the services of his Church, and to conform in offering up prayer to the present ordinary practice of the Church.[11]

It is said that Dr. Lee put his book aside only after he had memorized the prayers it contained, which thereafter, without using the book, he continued to recite Sunday after Sunday in Old Greyfriars'.

But that was not the end of his case. Legal proceedings were begun against him again in 1865 and dragged on till 1867. The day before the Assembly was to open, however, Dr. Lee fell from his horse, the victim of a paralytic stroke, and within the year he was dead. No determination was ever reached, therefore, regarding these new complaints. The dramatic suddenness of Dr. Lee's death left unresolved many of the questions which his career in Old Greyfriars' had raised. But he had succeeded in reopening permanently the liturgical question in the Church of Scotland.

The next stage in the story was to be in the control of more cautious hands. In 1858, the year after the reopening of Old Greyfriars', a curious little book was published in Scotland. It was obviously a hasty production and was entitled:

> Presbyterian Liturgies with Specimens of Forms of Prayer for Worship as used in the continental Reformed and American Churches.

Although like so much of the liturgical literature of the period it was published anonymously, we now know that the author was Andrew Bonar, minister of the Canongate in Edinburgh.

Apparently Bonar was of a double mind about the liturgical situation in Scotland. He was convinced that liturgical restoration was necessary and represented a movement that was here to stay. But he was concerned about the liberal theology expressed in Dr. Lee's forms. He rushed into print to assure his brethren that liturgy need not be liberal but that it had an honorable place in the theological history of the Reformed churches. Fearing that Dr. Lee's open latitudinarianism could prejudice the whole future of liturgical revival in the Scottish Church, Bonar was anxious to prove that it need not be so.

And what was his principal evidence? Baird's *Eutaxia*, as edited by Binney. But there is even more. Not only did Bonar make generous quotations from Baird, he included the liturgy for both the Lord's Supper and the Burial of the Dead from the revised *Liturgy* of the American Reformed Dutch Church which had been published only the year before in 1857. To demonstrate his complete familiarity with the American liturgical scene, he added some draft prayers for the festivals of the Christian year which had recently appeared in the *Mercersburg Review* as specimens of the liturgical studies of the American German Reformed Church. It can thus be argued that the liturgical activity of the various American Reformed churches was responsible for the development of similar activities in Great Britain.

Bonar's plea for a Scottish liturgy was especially urgent, he felt, in view of the needs of Presbyterians in the armed forces and in distant colonial lands where the services of a minister were not available. The General Assembly had appointed a committee to study this matter as early as 1849, and Bonar was anxious that the report should not brush these needs aside but seek to meet them with some liturgical forms.

The committee reported in 1858, the very year in which Bonar's book was published. Its report led to the publication, with the authorization of the Assembly, of *Prayers for Social and Family Worship*. Judged by present standards, it was not a great piece of work. But as the first official liturgical publication of the Church of Scotland since the Westminster Assembly it is certainly deserving of mention.

Events now began to move rapidly. On January 31, 1865 a small group met to form the Church Service Society. Scarcely enough in number to fill an elder's pew in one of the Glasgow churches, the group took as its object

> the study of the liturgies, ancient and modern, of the Christian Church, with a view to the preparation and ultimate publication of certain forms of prayer for public worship, and services for the administration of the sacraments.[12]

Despite the hard work required of its membership, the Society grew in both numbers and influence until it reported a membership of 669 in 1892. In 1867, just two years after its organization, the Church Service Society published *Euchologion*, a book of prayers intended for use with the scheme of the *Westminster Directory*.

Euchologion was an instant success; by 1884 it had reached its fifth edition. In addition to forms of prayer for morning and evening worship each Sunday of a month, it contained liturgies for the two sacraments, marriage, and burial of the dead. It also included a lectionary, prayers for the Christian festivals (the observance of which thus began in Scotland for the first time since the Reformation), and other miscellaneous materials. The length of the prayers and their Victorian verbosity would make them unsuitable for use today. But in its own time *Euchologion* represented a high liturgical achievement which was of great influence on later liturgies in the Scottish Church.

The formation of the Church Service Society awakened similar interests in the other Scottish Presbyterian churches. The United Presbyterian Devotional Association was formed in 1882. In 1891 it published *Presbyterian Forms of Service,* a somewhat slighter volume than *Euchologion.* The Free Church Public Worship Association came into being in 1891, producing *A New Directory for Public Worship* in 1898. When the United Free Church was formed, these two organizations were combined in 1901 to become the Church Worship Association of the United Free Church. At the reunion of 1929 the Church Worship Association joined forces with the Church Service Society, which still continues its program of study and publication.

That place is somewhat less than formerly, however, by reason of the fact that the publication of liturgical forms has once again become an official task of the Church and not one for private associations. *The Book of Common Order* (note the revival of Knox's title, the last official liturgy of the Church) which appeared in 1940 once again gave the Scottish Church an official standard for public worship. It could be added that it gave the Presbyterian Church in this country a semiofficial one, for the most recent edition of the *Book of Common Worship* (1946) is in many respects a copy of the Scottish original. That judgment may have to be changed when the new edition, which at this writing is being prepared, makes its appearance.

Before leaving *Euchologion* and its successors, we should notice the part which American liturgical work played in its formation. Dr. George Washington Sprott of North Berwick was the chairman of the committee to prepare it. Perhaps he had read Bonar or perhaps his experience in Canada as a young man had given him some knowledge of American developments. But he knew them. In his own lectures, *The Worship and Offices of the Church of Scotland,* he gave a bibliography of useful liturgies which, presumably, had been consulted in the compilation of *Euchologion.* In that list can be found not only the liturgies of the American Dutch and German churches, Baird's *Eutaxia,* but even the Liturgy of the French Protestant Church of Charleston, South Carolina, the American version of Ostervald's Neuchâtel liturgy.[18]

What is more, Sprott also acknowledged that much of the

Eucharistic prayer in *Euchologion* had been taken from the American German Reformed Liturgy.[14] There is an interesting sequel to that acknowledgment. When in 1873 the American Dutch Reformed Church once again revised its liturgy, the Eucharistic prayer which was used was largely borrowed from *Euchologion,* which had originally been borrowed from the German Church (and which, if the facts be known, the German Church had largely borrowed from the Catholic and Apostolic Church, a group of which more will be said later). This kind of liturgical exchange, which had taken place earlier in the sixteenth century, was a hopeful sign that the Reformed churches, after years of isolation, were beginning again to find each other.

American liturgical developments may have played a part in another European revival, though this case is somewhat less certain. In 1850 a young Swiss student spent a year in this country, living in the old Huguenot town of New Rochelle, New York, with Dr. Robert Baird, the father of the author of *Eutaxia.* It is also interesting to notice that among the friends he made was Dr. Bethune, the liturgical leader in the Dutch Reformed Church.

When he returned to Europe, Eugène Bersier became the leader of liturgical revival in the Reformed Church in France. His interest in the liturgy has often been explained through his family connections. Benoit says of him:

> . . . he had English blood in his veins through his mother, so that the Anglican liturgy was not without influence on the liturgical developments in the Reformed Church.[15]

Very possibly so. But is it fanciful to suppose that a year spent in this country in the company of men who were leaders in the Reformed and Presbyterian liturgical revival was also a factor which influenced the young Bersier?

Though he was Swiss, Bersier's name is associated with the city of Paris, where he spent his entire ministry. His reputation as a pulpit orator was international. L'Eglise de l'Etoile was virtually built for him in 1874, and fashionable Paris crowded it whenever he was in the pulpit. But unlike most pulpit orators, Bersier was also genuinely concerned about the liturgy. The form of service which he introduced in l'Etoile became almost as celebrated as his sermons.

It was published in 1876, and in the introduction Bersier gave some of his reasons for liturgical reform.

1. Since too exclusive a part has been given heretofore to instruction under the form of preaching so that the sermon has absorbed everything else, to give back to worship itself, to common prayers and adoration their proper place.

3. Instead of giving the congregation the role of passive spectators, save for the singing, to permit them, by means of responses, to share directly in the worship itself. . . .

6. To affirm the close solidarity which unites the church of the present with that of the past, to introduce into public worship some of the elements of edification which antiquity has left us so that the voices of believers of all ages may be united with those of believers to-day. . . .

7. To restore to the Holy Supper the central place which it must have in Christian worship of which it is the loftiest expression; to return, at this point, to the true and primitive teaching of the Reformed Church.[16]

Bersier's *Liturgie* was a very complete prayer book of 354 pages, including a musical supplement with his sister-in-law's settings for the various liturgical responses which he had used in his services. These responses showed an Anglican influence which was also revealed in the position of the great prayer before the sermon. Complete prayers and lessons for the Christian year were also included. Some of the prayers were Bersier's own composition and show a rare skill. Here is a single example:

O Christ, Who wast rich, yet became poor for our sake; King of glory, Who didst will to become the man of sorrows; teach us to serve Thee in the person of our poor and weak brethren, suffering and scorned, lest we be among those to whom Thou shalt say at the last day, "Depart from Me."[17]

All of the prayers, including the great prayer of thanksgiving and intercession, were done in the Anglican manner as a series of collects to which the people made response.

Encouraged by the response which his liturgy received in his own congregation in Paris, Bersier accepted the invitation of the General Synod to prepare a modified version of it for consideration as the official liturgy of the French Reformed Church. This volume appeared in 1888 with a very complete historical introduction, as well as an extended commentary on each of the services. Incidentally, in the introduction Bersier acknowledged that he had not known Ostervald's preface (though he had known his liturgy) when he had written the introduction to his own liturgy in 1876. The similarity of the two documents is quite remarkable.

Bersier's projected liturgy of 1888 sacrificed many of the Anglicanisms of the liturgy prepared for l'Etoile. The responses have all gone; the series of collects has been replaced by the traditional prayer after the sermon, which has been restored not only as to language but to its old position. All of the materials for the Christian year are still included. In the Eucharistic liturgy the traditional Genevan prayer has been substituted for Bersier's, though the preface and Sanctus are still retained as an introduction to it. These alterations had been made in the hope that they might make the projected liturgy more palatable to the majority of French churches. That was not to be the case, however. Yet even though Bersier's liturgy was officially rejected, it exercised a tremendous influence on the worship of the French Church. Twentieth-century liturgical developments in that church remain greatly in Bersier's debt.

The half century from 1850 to 1900 saw so many liturgical experiments and suggestions, especially among the Reformed and Presbyterian churches of this country, that a discussion of all of them would occupy an entire book—and a fascinating book it would be. Once the process had begun, it never seemed to stop. A small library could be made of the liturgical books produced in this country during that time.

We can mention only a few. In 1866 Dr. Abraham Rynier Van Nest, a Dutch Reformed minister who had served the American Church in Florence, published the *American Union Prayer Book*. Compiled from the liturgies of both the Anglican and the Dutch Reformed churches, in its day it was thought to be a model for future ecumenical worship.

Someone should fully explore the story of St. Peter's Presbyterian Church in Rochester, New York, a congregation which was

organized to be a liturgical parish in the Presbyterian Church. I
have no information as to its success or failure, except to know
that it ultimately disappeared. But during its lifetime it produced
a variety of liturgical publications including a hymnal and a
prayer book.

It was an era also in which people made extreme, not to say
silly, proposals. McCrie records one such which was published
in Calcutta in 1890 by a Presbyterian layman. His proposals included, among other things, a service for Christ Mass and suggestions for new vestments—cassock, surplice, purple velvet stole,
and a scarlet merino hood—to replace the somber Geneva gown.[18]
But though there were a few eccentrics, as there are in all new
movements, for the most part the liturgical recovery of the
Gothic age was carried on by sober and serious-minded men who
studied hard and knew what they wanted.

To a surprising degree they got it. To realize how much which
we take for granted we owe to these liturgical pioneers of the
Gothic age, we have only to imagine what worship was like in
our churches before they came on the scene. No stained-glass
windows, no Gothic churches, no choirs, vested or otherwise, no
responses, in many instances no organs—this is only a hasty cata-
logue of their innovations or, as they would have preferred,
restorations. And we should still have to mention the improved
decorum of public worship, the new significance of the Christian
year, the new importance of Holy Communion.

For better or worse, we also owe to them the changed architectural setting of our worship in many places. Here we cannot
always be grateful. Caught up in the fashions of the Gothic age,
they unquestioningly imitated what they took to be medievalism.
Chancels were divided with no thought given to the fact that a
medieval chancel bore no relation to the needs of a worshiping
congregation in a Reformed church. Lovely old Georgian meetinghouses were disastrously darkened in decoration and filled up
with bad stained glass. Apparently the Gothic mind thought that
religion was a somber business. The old white pews with their
cherry or mahogany tops were replaced by walnut or golden oak,
usually stained.

A typical example can be seen in one lovely old town church (now partially restored) which had been built at the end of the eighteenth century by a local architect who gave it the slightest flavor of Baroque. In the mid-nineteenth century it was painted a chocolate color from the top of its twin towers to the base of its foundation. This was done to simulate the then fashionable brownstone. All the clear glass windows were replaced with a hideous green, and the finished product was solemnly described as a fine example of the Romanesque!

Almost every town in the states along the Atlantic coast can show some such example. It would be unfair to blame the liturgical revival of the Gothic age for all of them. But they were in many ways the result of the same spirit. And in no way did these revivalists leave a more lasting impression than in the way in which they gave even twentieth-century man an "image" of what a church should look like. Whenever the modern American turns away from a contemporary church in horror, saying, "But it doesn't even look like a church!", he is paying unwitting tribute to the Gothic age.

For all that, the nineteenth century was in many ways the golden age in the liturgical life of the Reformed churches. In a recent *Annual* of the Church Service Society in Scotland a writer has lamented that the liturgy is no longer the controversial thing that it then was. Study groups, publications, conferences, were then the order of the day. And while liturgical interests often involved battle, as witness the curious activities of Jacob Primmer in Scotland, these men relished a fight and gave as good as they got.[19]

The unfortunate thing was that their work fell into the hands of a generation that was less well educated theologically. Scottish pioneers like Sprott and Leishman knew the liturgical history and theology of the Reformed churches. Americans like Bethune or Baird were proudly aware of the tradition in which they stood. Bersier's introduction to his liturgical project is still a mine of information about worship in France and the French cantons of Switzerland.

But once the way had been cleared, those who walked in it

seem to have been more interested in aesthetics than in theology. It was often easier for them to imitate the Anglican churches than dig for buried treasure in their own back yards. The historical and the theological began to mean less and less as the demands of the psychological and the aesthetic loomed larger.

To realize this, one has only to try to make a liturgical bibliography in the Reformed and Presbyterian tradition. The nineteenth century can provide scores of titles; the years since the Second World War as many if not more. But the years in between show only a scant handful. The liturgical revival of the Gothic age was apparently not able to sustain itself once the initial gains had been made.

A second criticism of the movement would be about its relation to the layman, although information here is somewhat difficult to gather. But reading the history of the nineteenth century certainly gives the impression that the liturgy was so exclusively a clerical pastime that, with exceptions like Lord Sands in Scotland, it was a pother that was going on over the layman's head and one in which he had no great interest.

We can be sure that many of them did not like it. The pietist, remembering the close alliance between liturgy and liberalism, was always suspicious. In fact, he is still. In how many places is the minister who is interested in liturgy met with the implied or overt accusation that he has lost his gospel?

But even in those congregations in which the liturgical movement was accepted, for many laymen it seems to have been just another way of doing things which, if the minister wanted it, they would tolerate. Gunning records an interesting observation about Bersier's own congregation in Paris, one of the most liturgical Reformed churches of the century.

> Different visitors to Paris have assured me that even in Bersier's church, under the leadership of this earnest man himself, many come in only after the liturgical part of the service is ended, while others sit through it with obvious boredom.[20]

If that was true in Paris in a congregation which had one of the great preachers of the century in its pulpit, what must have hap-

pened in many other congregations with ministers of ordinary
stature?

The obvious conclusion is that there was a real failure to give
instruction in the meaning of worship, to explain to the layman
what all these improvements and additions to the service signi-
fied. Surely the laudable intention to make them more than spectators, as Bersier said, to make them active participants in the
service, involved more than giving them a few responses to sing
or teaching them to say Amen at the end of the prayers. It should
have involved nothing less than their complete re-education as to
the meaning of their membership in the body of Christ.

That that never happened and was never intended to happen
is indicated by the simple fact that almost all of the liturgies in
question were published as guides for the pulpit, not as books for
the pew. They were intended to guide the minister in the enriched conduct of public worship, to save him from the erratic
theology of improvers like Dr. Lee. They were never meant to
guide the layman in the development of his ministry as a member
of Christ's redeemed people. Even the *Book of Common Order*
of the Church of Scotland, a communion of well over one million
adults, had at last report sold something like twenty thousand
copies.

But this failure leads directly to a third criticism. The movements of the Gothic age were responsible for all kinds of improvements in our worship for which we should be grateful. But
they never faced the basic question of the subject with which
they were dealing. They never asked what a liturgy is or how it
involves a congregation. Despite almost universal recognition of
the necessity for more frequent celebrations of the Eucharist and
some real progress in that direction (and some more apparent
than real, as for example the celebration of the sacrament at odd
hours for the spiritually elite), there is no basic discussion of the
relation of Word to Sacrament, no discussion of the meaning of
the Word or the Eucharist except in language that repeated the
time-honored confessional phrases.

In the Gothic age the Table had begun to recover some of the
significance it had lost to the pulpit. In many churches it was at

least made a permanent symbol. But the seventeenth- and eighteenth-century idea of the liturgy as something done by the minister for the people still largely prevailed. The chief concern was to see that he did it better. And that, of course, was something. But we are still suffering from the fact that in the recovery of our liturgical life aesthetics so quickly usurped the place of theology.

The Gothic age recovered the forms which preceding centuries had abandoned. But the liturgy was still only an orderly and impressive, not to say pretty, way of doing things. In the Gothic age even the Unitarians became liturgical and produced a prayer book. The Reformed churches still had to discover the theology of the liturgy.

But even in the Gothic age, movements in that direction were beginning. The theological foundation which could adequately support the liturgical structure was being laid. While most liturgical minds were busy improving what we do in worship, some were beginning to ask why we do it. Were it not for them and their question, we should have little or nothing to improve.

IV

THE LITURGY FINDS A THEOLOGY

When we begin to trace out the ways in which in the nineteenth century a theological basis was provided for the liturgy, we soon discover at almost every turn the shadowy figure of one of the greatest heresiarchs any Reformed church ever produced. There are many indeed who would maintain that Edward Irving was never guilty of heresy, that if there was any heresy it was on the part of the Scottish presbytery which deposed him in 1833. They will admit that he was guilty of both affectation and exaggeration, that he lacked discrimination, that he was easily imposed upon by less talented people than himself. But in his understanding of the doctrine of the Incarnation, he was more orthodox than the Church of Scotland.

It is unfortunate that if anyone knows Edward Irving's name today he is likely to know it in connection with speaking in tongues. The common opinion of Irving is that he was a raving religious fanatic. It was an opinion that was held soon after his death.

> Thinking his faults great and terrible, his mischief done to the churches . . . great and infinite . . . his motives awfully mixed with arrogance, folly, love of popularity, and multifarious selfishness, I do mean to condemn him. . . . If pride, disappointment, and intensified study, or living remorse, had actually cracked his knowledge-box and made him *non compos mentis*, and so irresponsible, so be it. It was the only possible apology that could be made for him.[1]

For the fact is that despite some of the bizarre things in Irving's collected works and their almost incredible verbosity, he broke new ground in the theology of the Reformed churches. Even the brief anthology that his recent biographer, Dr. Whitely, has made as an appendix to his little book *The Blinded Eagle* indicates that Edward Irving was one of the pioneers in the recovery of a doctrine of church, sacraments, and ministry in the Reformed churches. If the outburst of glossolalia in his London congregation had not so tragically altered his career, how different his story and that of the Scottish Church might have been!

It was apparently during his ministry in London (we have scant record of his thinking during his Glasgow days when he was Dr. Chalmers' assistant) that Irving became convinced of what he aptly called "the infidelity of Evangelicalism." To understand what he meant by this phrase, we have to remind ourselves of the typically orthodox position of the Reformed churches in the opening years of the nineteenth century. The theological historian will know that it contained large elements of pietism and even a trace of rationalism. But it had come to be the orthodox Reformed stance.

The following description is of New England Calvinism. But it could just as well describe any of the Reformed churches of the time, British, American, or Continental.

> Though the Divinity of Christ was firmly held, the wide-reaching significance of the Incarnation was little apprehended; and though the facts of His Resurrection and Ascension were articles of faith, their bearings upon His present priesthood and upon His future kingship were only dimly seen. . . . The great doctrinal topic of the pulpit was the way in which His death was related to the forgiveness of sin. . . . The great channel of His operations was the preached word, not ordinances or sacraments. The sermon was therefore the centre of interest, and the other parts of the service were regarded as introductory and subordinate. . . .
>
> It was generally held that at the Lord's table the communicants ate and drank as a mere commemorative act—a vivid way of bringing the Lord and His work to remembrance.[2]

It was in this kind of setting that Irving did his theological thinking. Beginning with the Incarnation, he came to believe that the common scheme of Reformed orthodoxy, though it had all the essential parts, had them in the wrong perspective. The result of this false perspective was that the whole center of the gospel had been shifted from God and his mighty acts to man and his faith. Perhaps it was his fondness for Anglican authors like Richard Hooker that persuaded Irving of the necessity for a theological reorientation. But it was significant that he thought he had come to it through his study of the old Scots Confession, the standard of faith which the Westminster Confession had superseded.

> This, the Confession of the Protestant Church of Scotland, is mighty upon the sacraments, that strongest hold of faith, which superstition is ever endeavoring to possess, and infidelity to undermine. . . . It was this . . . which delivered me from the infidelity of Evangelicalism, which denies any gift of God either in the work of Christ, or in the sacraments, or anywhere, until we experience it to be within ourselves; making God a mere promiser until we become receivers. . . . The true doctrine of the sacraments will always strike this infidelity upon the head.[3]

His two long series of lectures on the sacraments were the result of Irving's new concern. That irate listener who interrupted him once in Glasgow to say, "Ye're an awfu' man, Mr. Irving. They say you preach a Roman Catholic baptism and a Mohammedan heeven!"[4] was in some ways a more acute observer than some of his critics in the presbytery. For what was it from which Edward Irving felt that he had been delivered? In the last analysis it was the subjectivity of the theological approach in which he had been brought up. So long as that persisted, there could be no liturgy that was anything more than a "nice" way of doing things, for there was really no Church and therefore no sacraments. But once that subjectivity had been struck upon the head, a whole new range of possibilities opened up, most of which Irving did not live to explore.

We must not exaggerate the importance of Edward Irving in the development of a Reformed theology of the church. But his importance is often underestimated. Liturgical historians all point out the great significance of the Liturgy of the Catholic and Apostolic Church, the strange denomination that gathered about Irving after his expulsion by the presbytery, though he had little to do with it. We shall have occasion to point it out ourselves later. But too often they pass over the significance of Irving's own theological pioneering.

Irving's hammer blows at the "infidelity of Evangelicalism" were the beginning of the end for the hitherto dominant interpretation of Reformed theology in pietist terms. He was the first to assert in vigorous terms that the foundation of the church is in the objective deed of God, manifested in baptism, and not in the subjective choice of the believer. Until that foundation had been laid, no real doctrine of the church, to say nothing of its liturgical life, was possible.

When we consider the pioneers of a liturgical theology in the Reformed churches of the nineteenth century it is amazing how many of them looked to Edward Irving as one of their primary inspirations, whether they had read his works or knew him only by reputation. J. H. Gunning in Holland several times thought of joining the Catholic and Apostolic Church. John MacLeod of Govan in Scotland was thought of as an Irvingite. John Williamson Nevin of this country was influenced by the current of Irving's thought. For it was Irving who had begun to clear away the pietism and individualism which had become so dominant in Reformed theology, making clear that they were not implicit in the original Reformed confessions of faith but were a later growth, or, if you like, a heresy. It was Irving who quarried the stones which other men could use to lay the foundation for a Reformed theology of the liturgy.

Whether Edward Irving would have had any interest in the liturgical expression of his theological ideas had he lived is impossible to say. The community which was gathered after his expulsion from the Scottish Church certainly did. It is not true that Irving would have opposed the liturgical developments of the Catholic and Apostolic Church, as his community came to be known. That has sometimes been said. But all of the theological ideas which that liturgy embodies are powerfully present in Irving's writings.

A consideration of the Liturgy of the Catholic and Apostolic Church really lies outside our field of study. But we may say in passing that among the liturgies of Christendom it would certainly belong in the very first rank. That a small group of British laymen could have produced a liturgical document of such high order is a tribute to the intensive study of liturgical material from East and West which they made. Though it suffers from a prolixity which reminds one of Irving himself, the Catholic and Apostolic liturgy will repay careful study. As the Catholic and Apostolic community continues to diminish and its places of worship one by one are closed, it is something to know that its liturgical testimony has influenced the life of many other churches.[5]

The story of that influence begins at a point thousands of miles away from London or Albury, where the Catholic and Apostolic liturgy was compiled. In 1849 the Synod of the German Reformed Church in this country appointed a committee to revise its liturgy, a sadly mangled version of the old Palatinate liturgy. The two leading members of the committee were professors at the little seminary in Mercersburg, Pennsylvania, Dr. John Williamson Nevin and Dr. Philip Schaff. Nevin shortly grew discouraged by the task and resigned the chairmanship, which went to Schaff. though Nevin continued on the committee. Their work was completed in 1857 with the publication of the so-called *Provisional Liturgy*, which was revised in 1866 and published as the *Order of Worship*.

To look at either the earlier or later form of this liturgy, remembering the time and place in which it appeared, is to ask how one of the more provincial Reformed churches, ministering largely to a rural constituency in Pennsylvania, could have produced one of the finest liturgies of any Reformed church in the world. The answer is to be found in the ability of the two professors who largely influenced the committee. But we must still ask where they obtained their familiarity with liturgical material to the extent indicated by their completed work.

A Swiss by birth, Philip Schaff had been educated in Germany.

He was thus in close association with the United Evangelical Church. Probably he had some acquaintance with the revival of Lutheran liturgics which was so strongly felt in the United Church in the first half of the nineteenth century. He also had some acquaintance with the Oxford Movement, gathered from a visit he made there on his way to take up his duties in America.

An interesting item is to be found in his correspondence during a visit to Britain in 1854 when the work of his committee was in full swing and, as we learn from one of the members, Schaff was prosecuting it with great energy. Writing to his wife, he said,

> Sunday I spent the greater part of the day with the Irvingites. In the morning I found their beautiful Gothic church in Gordon Square, the first of the seven churches of London, thronged with devout worshippers. The Lord's Supper was administered with great solemnity, an imposing ceremonial, many hundreds communing. . . . The liturgy is very beautiful. I dined with the angel of the church, Mr. Heath, meeting his large and amiable family. . . . Then at four I attended the service designed for the congregation and at seven the service of the evangelists for outsiders. The service this morning, I believe, was the most beautiful and perfect liturgical service I have yet attended.[6]

This visit to Gordon Square, for which arrangements must have been made in advance, would indicate some previous knowledge of the Irvingites. That may have come from his studies in Berlin, for the movement was by no means confined to Britain. Or, as we shall see presently, it may have come from his colleague in Mercersburg, Dr. Nevin. Certainly the day spent in attending services and visiting with Mr. Heath was in strong contrast to his usual hit-and-run visits to all the leading preachers he could take in on a given Sunday. The letter indicates more than a fleeting impression; something more like a strong current of influence. We can safely assume that Schaff returned to Mercersburg with a copy of the Catholic and Apostolic liturgy in his luggage.

The background of John Williamson Nevin had been much less cosmopolitan. A graduate of Princeton in 1826, he had served for ten years on the faculty of the young Presbyterian Seminary in Pittsburgh (Alleghany City). By a set of curious chances he had come from there to Mercersburg in 1840. A growing distaste for the crude methods and implied theology of revivalism had given him a concern with the "infidelity of Evangelicalism." His association with Schaff on the Mercersburg faculty greatly stimulated that concern. Increasingly the articles from his pen were on the "Church Question."

The war of pamphlets, heresy trials, and general ecclesiastical ructions which Nevin and Schaff provoked in the German Reformed Church would be a study in itself.[7] Our interest at the moment, however, is in a series of articles on the Eucharist which appeared in 1846 over the signature of W. W. A. The author was William Watson Andrews, minister of the Congregational Church in Kent, Connecticut. Though a Congregationalist, he was greatly under the influence of the Catholic and Apostolic Church, which indeed he entered in 1849.

It was the purpose of Andrews' articles to endorse certain articles which Nevin had published on the objectivity of the real presence in the sacrament. The point, however, is not Andrews' defense of Nevin but rather the fact that it was through Andrews that Nevin made the acquaintance of Irvingism. It would seem likely that this acquaintance was more in the realm of theology than of liturgy. For in the long dispute which followed in the German Church, Nevin was usually the theologian and Schaff the liturgist.

Assuming an acquaintance of both men with the theology and liturgy of the Catholic and Apostolic Church, let us examine their work, beginning with the liturgy. Even a casual comparison of the Catholic and Apostolic *Liturgy* with the German Reformed *Order of Worship* will reveal the dependence of the American liturgy on the British original. The order for Holy Communion provides a good illustration.

Both liturgies begin with the invocation of the Trinity followed by a confession of sin. With only a few verbal changes, the German Reformed confession is identical with the Catholic and Apostolic original. The Absolution which follows in each service is different since the German Reformed has used the form from the old Palatinate Liturgy, one of the few forms from the Reformation which it has preserved.

In the rest of the service down to the offertory there are some changes in the sequence of items and the German Reformed liturgy is somewhat shorter than the Catholic and Apostolic. The Offertory prayers from the Catholic and Apostolic liturgy are omitted in the German Reformed, though it retains the so-called Prayer of the Veil, with a few verbal changes.

The great Eucharistic thanksgiving is similar in both, though in the German Reformed version Schaff has made use of some Eastern material which is not found in the Catholic and Apostolic rite. Both end the thanksgiving with the singing of the *Sanctus* (Holy, holy, holy, etc.) and *Benedictus Qui Venit* (Blessed is He that cometh in the name of the Lord).

The consecration which follows is the point at which the German Reformed committee showed its theological independence. Probably the prayer was the work of Nevin. As a theologian who had made an extensive study of Calvin's Eucharistic ideas, he would have wanted an accurate statement of the Calvinist position.

> Almighty God, our heavenly Father, send down, we beseech Thee, the powerful benediction of Thy Holy Spirit upon these elements of bread and wine, that being set apart now from a common to a sacred and mystical use, they may exhibit and represent to us with true effect the body and blood of Thy Son, Jesus Christ; so that in the use of them we may be made, through the power of the Holy Ghost, to partake really and truly of His blessed life, whereby only we can be saved from death, and raised to immortality at the last day.[8]

Whatever Nevin's prayer may lack in literary and liturgical grace it makes up for in theological accuracy. The irony is that this very prayer, so nicely Calvinistic in its theology, was cited by some of Nevin's opponents in evidence of his Romanizing tendencies.

The remainder of the two liturgies runs quite parallel. The Mercersburg rite is generally briefer, omitting much of the commemoration of the faithful departed. The post-Communion prayer, the use of the *Te Deum* as a post-Communion thanksgiving, and the final blessing are the same in both liturgies.

Even this brief outline should help to make clear what a startling development in Reformed worship the *Order of Worship* was. Small wonder that it was the occasion for a liturgical battle in the German Reformed Church, lasting almost a quarter of a century. During that time congregations were split, families were sundered, rival educational institutions were founded. The German Church found itself cut off from fellowship with almost every other Reformed and Presbyterian body in the country.

Before we leave the Catholic and Apostolic *Liturgy* and its influence, it should be noted that its influence was by no means confined to the *Order of Worship,* although it was perhaps the strongest in that case. As has already been noted, it was of considerable influence in the formation of the Scottish *Euchologion* and so, indirectly, in the making of the revised liturgy of the American Dutch Church. Since translations of the Catholic and Apostolic *Liturgy* existed in both French and German, it was of primary importance in the churches of these countries as well. No one can really understand the liturgical revival in the Reformed churches of the nineteenth century who is not acquainted with the *Liturgy* of the Catholic and Apostolic Church.

But to return to Mercersburg. What made the liturgical movement there remarkable was not the *Order of Worship,* despite its high degree of liturgical skill. It was rather the fact that it was the first liturgy in the Reformed Church to articulate a theology. Indeed, it was at Mercersburg that there was worked out, often in the heat of battle, for the first time in the Reformed churches what could be called a theology of the liturgy. That part of the story takes us to John Williamson Nevin.

Though we have already mentioned Nevin's acquaintance with the Catholic Apostolic Church through Andrews, it should be pointed out that the tendency of his own thinking had been moving in this direction for some years. While he was still in Pittsburgh a study of Neander, the German church historian, and the chance reading of one of the Oxford *Tracts for the Times* had started Nevin thinking about the doctrine of the church. His conflict with the revivalism practiced in the local Reformed congregation in Mercersburg had stimulated his thinking still further.

When Philip Schaff came to Mercersburg in 1844, fresh from those very circles in Germany in which much of this new ecclesiology was being produced, he found in Nevin a colleague who was ready to move with him. But though Schaff provided much of the material and information, the real formulation of it, to say nothing of its defense, was left to Nevin, aided somewhat in later years by his favorite pupil, Henry Harbaugh.

It is important to notice that Nevin's concern in this movement began not with liturgy but with theology. Whatever he may have felt about the liturgical inadequacy of his church, he had no interest in liturgical improvement as such. In fact, at several points in the story he seems to have been quite shy of it. First concerned with a theology of the church, he moved from there to a consideration of the sacraments, especially the Eucharist.

Nevin's various pamphlets and articles on the church were followed in 1846 by his major work, the *Mystical Presence; a Vindication of the Reformed or Calvinistic Doctrine of the Holy Eucharist.* Though the sequence cannot be pressed too literally, it is important to notice it. The order of consideration was the doctrine of the church, then the doctrine of the Eucharist. Only after he had worked out his theology of the sacraments was he ready to move on to the liturgical question itself. For Nevin the liturgy was not an independent discipline but a consequence of, if not a part of, the theology of the sacraments.

But perhaps the theology of the church was not the central point in Nevin's thinking after all. It would perhaps be more accurate to say that for him, as for Irving, the central theology was that of the Incarnation. At a time when the person of Christ had been of little interest in Reformed theology (except in the curiously muddled discussion of it during the Unitarian controversy in New England), Nevin tried to reorient that theology toward the Incarnation.

> Jesus Christ Himself is the truth and reality of the Gospel which He came into the world to proclaim. It is not a message of salvation simply published by Him in an outward way. . . . His incarnation—the act of His coming in the flesh—was itself re-

demptive, and may be said to have included in itself, from the beginning, all that was needed for the full salvation of the world. It formed the true mediation between God and man, and served to bridge the awful chasm which before separated earth from heaven. What we call the atonement in its more special sense, as wrought out by His sufferings and death, was nothing more, after all, than the irresistible inevitable movement of the incarnation itself out to its own necessary end.

. . . in this sense, accordingly, we say of Christianity that it is made and constituted literally by the constitution of Christ's person; that it is thus not a doctrine primarily, nor a rule of life, but a grand historical fact.[9]

The logical deduction from such a center has been pointed out by one of the historians of Mercersburg theology.

The Mercersburg theologians were very much interested in the nature of the Christian Church. They did not believe that it was merely a gathering of men in a humanistic society, for they were sure that the Church was meant to play an essential part in the salvation of men by God. The Church, thus, was in some sense a supernatural organism . . . their concept of the nature of the Church was really a logical development from their faith and belief in Jesus Christ. . . . It was only logical for them to conclude . . . that the Church was the on-going incarnation of Jesus Christ on earth.[10]

The last phrase in the quotation is one which the Mercersburg theologians probably would not have used. But it is true that in their thinking the Church was a divine-human organism, the body of Christ, in and through which men found their salvation as they found their union with Him, the God-man, who is their Saviour.

The particular means of this union, appointed by Christ himself, was the Eucharist. In his *Mystical Presence*, Nevin suggested that the mystical union was the real center of Calvin's theology rather than the divine decrees. In this conclusion, incidentally, he seems to have anticipated such modern students of Calvin as Niesel and Torrance by more than a century. But not only are the sacraments the media of the mystical union, the sacraments alone can safeguard the Incarnation and keep it an ever-present reality.

Is the redemption of the Gospel, including all the benefits of

Christ's life and death, a concrete reality that holds in the force
of His living constitution as a perennial, indissoluble fact, the
new world which grace has made, and in this alone; or is it an
abstraction, which may be applied to men and appropriated by
faith in no connection with the *Life* by which it was originally
brought to pass? Our inward answer to all this must be ever
conditioned necessarily by our view of the Church; and finds its
exact measure always in our theory of the Holy Sacraments.[11]

It is the theology of the Incarnation, issuing in the church and
the sacraments, which Nevin maintained determined the nature
of Christian worship.

The last ground of all true Christian worship is the mystical
presence of Christ in the Holy Eucharist; all the parts of public
worship are inwardly bound together by their having a common
relation to the idea of a Christian altar.[12]

This basic theology could not, of course, determine the sequence of events in an order of service. But it did set the fundamental pattern. A liturgy must not be a "pulpit liturgy," as Nevin
called it, a collection of liturgical items for the guidance of the
minister. It must be what Nevin called an "altar liturgy." By that
phrase he meant a liturgy which would be the expression of
that mystical union which takes place between Christ and his
people in every act of Christian worship.

For Christian worship, as the Mercersburg authors repeatedly
pointed out, is not primarily our action but Christ's. Harbaugh
gave a clear statement in his address to the Tercentenary Con-
vention of 1863.

It [Christian worship] is the love of God, the grace of Christ,
the communion of the Holy Ghost, brought to us, the Church's
grace-bearing soil beneath us, all its motherly ministrations
around us and its constant communications from heaven upon
us, as being itself the kingdom, the power, and the glory of
heaven on earth—the tabernacle of God with men.[13]

From this general introduction he reached his conclusion.

From this brief exhibition of the true nature of cultus, we see
what are its centralities; the true high-priesthood of Christ in the
Church, the mediation of the Church, the priestly character of
the ministerial office, the altar in its true significance, the sacra-

ments, the church year. These do not merely belong to cultus; they are fundamental and central, forming its starting points, its basis and body, its vital organs, its indispensable supports and conservators. Cultus is mediation from Christ the Head to all His members; and these are the media through and by which the great mediation is realized for all God's worshiping people. Without these divine media, or without a believing sense of them on the part of the worshiper, let any one say how true Christian worship is possible.[14]

Worship, therefore, is objective. It is not a question of a subjective impression on the worshiper. Something happens in the liturgy; Christ is present and acts redemptively in his church. In Nevin's words,

The visible and invisible are bound together by the power of the Holy Ghost . . . in such sort that the presence of the one is, in truth, the presence of the other.[15]

In his article "The Theology of the New Liturgy," in which Nevin tried to meet the antisacramental objections of his critics, he summarized the case for the liturgy in this way:

The Liturgy stands as a protest and defence against this sacrilege. . . . It teaches that the value of Christ's sacrifice never dies, but is perennially continued in the power of His life. It teaches that the outward side of the sacrament is mystically bound by the Holy Ghost to its inward invisible side; so that the undying power of Christ's life and sacrifice are there for all who take part in it with faith. It teaches that it is our duty to appropriate this grace and bring it before God ("the memorial of the blessed sacrifice of His Son") as the only ground of our trust and confidence in His presence. All this the Liturgy teaches. Who will say that it wrongs, in so doing, the sacramental doctrine of the Reformed Church?[16]

In other words, the liturgy is the means by which the congregation on earth shares in the ministry of the living Christ in heaven. In him they are brought into the presence of God himself as with him they plead the merits of his Passion. This reference to the Eucharistic sacrifice becomes doubly significant when we recall that Nevin wrote the above words in 1867 about a question which is at the center of ecumenical liturgical discussion today.

There are some criticisms of Mercersburg which can be made. Their historical situation, for example, seems to have prevented the Mercersburg theologians from an adequate appreciation of Calvin's liturgical work. Harbaugh wrote, "Calvin's entire inward and outward life rendered him unapt for a churchly cultus,"[17] and blamed Calvin for all of the Puritanism which he held responsible for the liturgical decline in the Reformed churches.

More seriously, their reaction against Puritanism led the Mercersburg school to undervalue the Word. In their discussion of the activity of Christ in worship, neither Nevin or Harbaugh mentions the Word. They limit the discussion entirely to the Eucharist. That omission is significant. Though they were battling to restore the Table to a church which had come under the complete dominance of the pulpit, their failure to consider the Word indicates that they were still laboring under the scholastic idea of preaching as Biblical exposition and theological instruction. They had not recovered the Reformation idea of the Word itself mediating the presence of Christ, which was such an important element in early Reformed liturgics.

Other minor criticisms could be made. There is a certain Lutheranism in their attitudes of which they were themselves aware, though they preferred to call it "Melanchthonian." Nor are they entirely free from the romanticism which colored so much of the liturgical work of the nineteenth century. But when due account has been taken of these weaknesses, the Mercersburg movement must remain a significant landmark in the history of Reformed worship. Certainly it deserves to be better known not only in this country but in Britain and Europe as well. Not without reason has Nevin been ranked with Channing and Bushnell as one of the important theologians of nineteenth-century America.

The influence of Mercersburg on Reformed church worship was indirect. Reference has already been made to the part it played in the work of the Church Service Society in Scotland. Traces of it are to be found also in the later liturgical developments in both the Dutch Reformed and Presbyterian churches in this country. Sometimes there were direct borrowings from the *Order of Worship;* more often the influence of the movement in other churches was seen in the stimulation of liturgical study and publication.

One curious American production which followed in the wake of the Mercersburg movement was the *Presbyterian Book of Common Prayer*. It was published in 1864 (and reissued in 1897) under the editorship of Dr. Charles W. Shields, a member of the faculty of Princeton University. Essentially, Dr. Shields edited the emended *Book of Common Prayer* which had been submitted by the Presbyterians at the ill-starred Savoy Conference in 1661 after the restoration of Charles II.

But Dr. Shields had not intended to edit an antiquity. He was seeking to provide a prayer book for Presbyterian worship. The fact that his work enjoyed a second edition would seem to indicate that it was used. The supplementary treatise at the end of the book, though containing nothing new, was filled with liturgical common sense. But evidently the Princeton professor grew discouraged by Presbyterian prospects. History records that in later years Dr. Shields became an Episcopalian.

A development somewhat similar to the Mercersburg movement took place in the later nineteenth century in Scotland with the formation of the Scottish Church Society. Its leading spirits, men like Professor James Cooper of Glasgow, Dr. Henry Wotherspoon of Edinburgh, Dr. John MacLeod of Govan, and Dr. Thomas Leishman of Linton, had all been active in the Church Service Society. But they had felt that that organization, interested merely in forms of worship without any definite theological stance, did not go far enough. They were anxious for a society which would become involved in the basic theological questions of church, ministry, and sacraments. They represented, it need hardly be said, what is sometimes called the "High Church" point of view in the Church of Scotland.

While several members of the Society produced works of lasting merit, most notably Wotherspoon's *Religious Values in the Sacraments*, its sphere of influence continued small. Its interest was too often limited to the defense of Presbyterian ordination as against Anglican claims. In later years a tendency to antiquarianism limited its usefulness still further. One minister, for example, was refused membership because his congregation used individual cups in the celebration of the Eucharist.

It would be comforting to think that theological pioneering of the kind done by Irving or Nevin led directly to the promised land. But that would be naive. For the increasing interest of the time was not in the theology but in the psychology of worship. In America it pretty well came to dominate the liturgical life of the churches for more than half a century. Evidently there were signs of it rather early. In 1864 Dr. Shields had thought it necessary to say a word of protest against the tendency to "foster a depraved taste for the *impressive,* rather than the *expressive* forms of religious service."[18] But his protest went unheeded, as the increasing industrial wealth of both America and Britain made all kinds of things possible.

No impartial observer can deny that the fascination with the psychology of worship was historically a terrible revenge, especially in the Reformed churches, on a way of worship which had blithely ignored the congregation for centuries, leaving them to sit in motionless silence listening to one man do everything. Nor would anyone in his right mind want to surrender the real gains which the psychology of worship won for us. But we can lament the fact that in so many instances the first impulse to alter the traditional way of worship in the Reformed churches came from a psychology that had little or no theological orientation.

The results are most visible in the realm of church architecture. Visit any number of our village Bethels and what will you find? The first stage, of which many examples remain, involved lowering the pulpit virtually to the level of the congregation, making it a platform with a small desk for the Bible and the preacher's notes. The organ was then taken out of the rear gallery where it had been ever since it had been allowed in a Reformed church, its golden pipes strewn across the front of the church, with seats for a choir placed between the organ pipes and the pulpit platform. (It is amusing to hear this arrangement defended as Protestant because it is "pulpit-centered." It is often hard to tell what its center is.) What had been a building built to express the idea of a Church of the Word had now become an auditorium and concert hall.

But then the psychology of worship changed and this change had to be reflected. The visitor to the village Bethel today is likely to find that the pulpit desk has been shoved to one side and the tiny Communion Table moved to the center of the platform, decorated with the silver candlesticks from someone's dining room and one of those brass crosses which is turned out in distressing monotony by some enterprising manufacturer of church goods. Gone is the amusing variety of hats which once brightened the choir loft. The choir is now turned out smartly in purple gowns with cerise stoles. The minister has shed his cutaway and striped trousers. He now wears varying combinations of borrowed ecclesiastical plumage, a Geneva gown, an Anglican stole, a Lutheran pectoral cross, a Hathaway shirt and tie. The old harmonium has been recently replaced by a new electronic organ which, as the chart in the vestibule shows, has not quite been paid for.

Psychology has also dictated many changes in the worship. Sermons have shrunk in size and, some cynics would say, significance. But the service now contains numerous responses sung by the choir, often from the back of the church or, better still, behind closed doors. Extra time is consumed in processions and recessions. Many moving effects are achieved by that most important of modern liturgical devices, the rheostat. One great piece of ceremonial has been added. At a given point in the service the deacons come down the aisle with the precision of a military platoon to take up the offering. When it is returned, the minister, with great dignity, places it on the old marble-topped Communion Table which, except for this moment, stands unused forty-eight Sundays in the year. And yet for all this, if you asked the average member of the congregation why he had come, nine times out of ten he would reply, "To hear the sermon."

No one can deny that this reaction against the barrenness and bleakness, not to say slovenliness, of our Reformed way of worship was long overdue. But caught as we were for half a century in the clutches of a religious psychology which prostrated wor-

ship to become an instrument for the molding of moods and the
creating of impressions, we needed something to break through.
We still do, for in how many places is liturgy still dismissed as a
concern with decoration and millinery, about as remote from
theology as it is possible to get.

It is not possible to say just when the breakthrough came. It
cannot be credited directly to that neo-orthodoxy which was a
breakthrough in so many other directions. In fact, many of the
neo-orthodox theologians displayed a certain hostility to the
liturgical movement, although Karl Barth has some telling things
to say about worship in his *The Knowledge and Service of God*.
We should have to agree that the chief factor in the contemporary liturgical movement in the Reformed churches has been the
ecumenical one, hastened and even precipitated by the experience of two world wars.

But it must not be supposed that this liturgical concern was so
simple a matter as a kind of mutual exchange of goods. Sometimes
the impression is given that having met Anglicans, Lutherans, and
Eastern Orthodox in ecumenical discussions, we Reformed have
decided to borrow some of their liturgical treasures in exchange
for some of our theological ones—a kind of ecumenical lend-lease.
That there was a certain amount of that in the earlier days of the
ecumenical movement is probably true. Nor was it entirely a bad
thing. But if anyone supposes that our present liturgical concern
is nothing but imitated Anglicanism or rubbed-off Lutheranism,
he is very poorly informed.

For the fact is that this liturgical concern is just as strong in
the Anglican or Roman Catholic churches which have lived all
their lives with a highly developed liturgy as it is in the Reformed.
It cannot be explained more simply than by saying that it is the
result of the Bible. We are deeply indebted to the Biblical studies
which have greatly enriched our whole perspective on the liturgy.
But even more important than them is the fact that the churches
have all been reading the Scriptures freshly and freely, in the light
of their situation in the world in which they live.

And that reading of the Scriptures has raised many basic questions. What is the church? What is it here to do? How does it live?

Just as in the Mercersburg movement, these questions cannot be raised without bringing those who raise them face to face with the question of the liturgy. This is what has been happening in all the churches. It is what has been happening in the Reformed churches in France, Switzerland, the Netherlands, Scotland, and, one hopes, the United States.

Any of these individual church histories is a fascinating one. Their omission here is not to minimize their importance or ignore their results. But many of them are available in the English language. I have chosen the Church in the Netherlands to illustrate this modern development because it is probably the most dramatic. The Dutch Church was the last of the great Reformed churches to develop a liturgical interest and the most resistant to it when it did develop. In Scotland, Jacob Primmer was protesting the Romanism of the liturgical movement in the nineteenth century. In the Hague, ecclesiastical action to prohibit the use of kneeling benches in church was undertaken as recently as 1947.

All throughout our discussion of the various movements in the liturgical life of the Reformed churches in the nineteenth century there has been no mention of the Dutch Church, and for good reason. There was nothing to mention. When Gunning published his rather tentative discussion of worship in 1890, he was really breaking new ground. Abraham Kuyper, representing the other Reformed group in Holland, followed in 1897 with a series of articles which were later collected into a book. So completely had pietism and rationalism swept the field in the Netherlands that the only liturgical works published in the nineteenth century were historical commentaries on the old liturgical forms. Those same forms, unchanged in jot or tittle since 1619, were as ignored by the liberal party as they were reverenced by the orthodox and later by the Seceders.

The first liturgical service in the Netherlands was not held until November 12, 1911. On that Sunday, Domine Jan Gerretsen introduced some liturgical features into the worship of the old Kloosterkerk in the Hague. That was more than fifty years later than Dr. Lee's innovations in Edinburgh, almost forty years after Bersier introduced his liturgy in Paris.

But Gerretsen was a man of influence in the Dutch Church. In fact, as royal chaplain he baptized the present Queen of the Netherlands in 1909. His liturgy was a very modest one. At the beginning of the service he used the General Confession, Kyrie, Absolution, and Creed. But little as it was, it was apparently a moving experience for those who were present. One of them, Gerardus van der Leeuw, later to become one of the great liturgical scholars of the Dutch Church, described it in these words:

> It was the beginning of a new day. And whoever attended it can never forget the emotion when his own church began once again to pray and to confess in the form of the one holy Catholic Church of all the ages.[19]

A completely liturgical parish was founded in the Hague soon after this. The handsome Duinoordkerk in Scheveningen was built for this congregation in 1920 and became the shrine of the liturgical movement in the Netherlands until the Nazis destroyed it in 1945. It was in the Duinoordkerk in 1920 that the *Liturgische Kring* (the Liturgical Circle), a small group dedicated to the renewal of the liturgical life of the Dutch Church, was formed.

The first results of their studies appeared in 1923, a series of liturgical handbooks which was continued until its completion in 1930. These pamphlets, often showing great dependence on both Anglican and Roman Catholic developments, dealt with the various liturgical actions such as baptism, the Eucharist, marriage, and the Sunday service. In 1934 the *Kring* published *Eeredienst,* a complete Sunday service of both Word and Sacrament, and a *Handbook for Worship in the Dutch Reformed Church.*

These informal publications, though they differed little from similar early efforts in the Scottish and French churches, made an impression far beyond the small circle which had produced them. The *Kring's* success in arousing interest in the church was evidenced in 1933 when an official commission brought in the first report on the question of liturgy since 1816. Obviously the liturgy was beginning to be of interest to more than the little group which had been accused of making it a hobby.

Even more significant was the formation in 1938 of a second group, the *Kring Eeredienst* (the Worship Circle). This group, also devoted to the study of the liturgy, was formed from the liberal wing of the Dutch Church. In that house of many mansions there was by this time a feeling that *Liturgische Kring*, though working on a question of vital concern to the life of the church, was far too heavily influenced by both liturgical and theological tradition, was, in a word, too "High Church."

Conversations between these two groups, both without official recognition by the church, began in 1942 during the Nazi occupation, though each group continued its own work. *Kring Eeredienst* (the more liberal group) published its liturgy, the *Kanselboek*, in 1944. Though the title, *Pulpit Book*, indicates how far from liturgical concepts the group was, the contents indicate that the *Liturgische Kring* had not been without influence even in these more liberal circles.

The striking rebirth of the Dutch Church after the war is a thrilling one. It involved searching discussions about the church, the ministry, the church order, as the Reformed Church in the Netherlands sought to reorganize and re-establish its entire life. That meant, of course, facing the question of the liturgy. Two commissions were appointed in 1946 to deal with different aspects of the matter. In 1949 they were combined into one.

The first report of their work appeared in 1950. It was neither a liturgy nor a prayer book, nor even suggestions for liturgical improvements. It was a series of ten theses which, insofar as the Dutch words are capable of an English translation, were entitled *A Specimen Description*. Though they are too extensive for full quotation, we shall give the principal idea in each thesis. With few changes they represent those principles which have guided the liturgical revival in all of the Reformed churches on the continent.

   I   The congregation of Jesus Christ, gathered in the Name of her Lord, is called out of the world to His service. Her assembling together requires a foundation and a responsible order so that wherever it has pleased God to establish a remembrance of His Name, we may call upon that Name with reverence.

   II   The foundation of the gathering of the congregation is in the foundation of the whole Christian life, namely, that covenant which God has established with His people. . . . Just as surely as grace is there in the covenant before us . . . so surely is the coming together of the congregation a service of God to us. It is He Who addresses us with His word of grace and judgment, He Who grants us the once offered sacrifice of Christ, while we, gathered and blessed by Him, honor and glorify Him . . . in the hearing of His Word and the faithful receiving of His benefits with confession and thanksgiving, prayer and praise.

III   It is God Himself Who gives the congregation His blessed presence through preaching and sacrament. . . .

IV   The principal parts of the order for the gathering of the congregation can be read in Holy Scripture in so far as it instructs us in the practice of godliness. . . .

V   It pleases God that the service of the Word and the celebration of the Sacraments should take place in an officially ordered service. . . .

VI   Preaching, as the ministry of the Word, is done by exposition and application of Holy Scripture. . . .

VII   Although preaching . . . is directed to the whole world and involves all men, as the ministry of the Word it takes place within the congregation, pre-supposes Holy Baptism, and always invites to the Table of the Lord. It is never fully heard, understood, and received without these signs and seals which accompany and confirm it according to Christ's expressed institution. Preaching and sacrament together make a living and powerful Word of God in our midst through the working of the Holy Spirit.

VIII   Because preaching and the celebration of the sacraments are so closely bound together and used by the Spirit for the upbuilding of the body of Christ . . . the coming together of the congregation . . . may be understood as the pre-eminent place for the meeting of God with His own. . . .

IX   In the order of worship the lawful freedom and diversity of the Church is formed and limited by its catholic character and by its Reformation confession. . . .

X   It would be a blessing for this generation if the use of the Lord's Supper could again take its rightful place in the life of the congregation. . . . So should we do justice to that festival meal which sanctifies the Lord's Day. . . .[20]

A comparison of this declaration with Ostervald's manifesto, Bersier's preface, or the theological principles of Mercersburg will reveal that while there are great basic similarities, the twentieth century has added some new factors. They are chiefly in the repeated assertion that worship is an event, a meeting between

God and man in which something happens. While this understanding of worship may have been implicit in Mercersburg theology, these Dutch theses correct the one-sidedness of Nevin and Harbaugh by recognizing that Word as well as Sacrament is event. More accurately, Word and Sacrament together constitute *the* event of Christian worship. The only criticism which can be made of the *Specimen Description* is its omission of the eschatological character of Christian worship, an emphasis which is playing an increasingly important role in present liturgical thinking.

But to resume the narrative of events in Holland. These theses were a prelude to the appearance in 1955 of the *Dienstboek* (Service Book). Though it is subtitled *in ontwerp* (in the drafting stage) and its provisional character is indicated by the wide choices allowed for most occasions, choices which differ not only in liturgical construction but in theological point of view, it represents the first official liturgical action taken by the Dutch Church since 1619.

The preface explains that this book is only a stage in the liturgical development of the Dutch Church. At some future date the Synod will establish a definite form of worship for the church. In the meantime, ministers and consistories are obliged to make use of the forms contained in this book. Granted that such an obligation still allows a wide latitude, when we remember that in 1816 the Dutch Church had decided that a liturgical discussion would be a waste of energy since liturgies were only for the use of inexperienced ministers, we can see how greatly opinion has changed. While the new situation of the church and its ecumenical contacts have done much to bring about this change, we must not overlook the quiet and unofficial work of small groups like *Kring Eeredienst* and the *Liturgische Kring* which did so much to prepare the way.

The story of the French-speaking Reformed churches is somewhat similar. In the vicinity of Lausanne an informal group, *L'Eglise et Liturgie*, was founded more than thirty years ago for liturgical study and publication. Since each cantonal church retains its complete independence, in Switzerland the situation is a little more complicated than in Holland. But the leavening influence of *L'Eglise et Liturgie* has been evidenced in the publication of new liturgies for the churches of Geneva and Vaud. Most recently its influence can be seen in the new liturgy for the French churches in the Canton of Berne, which is the finest of the modern liturgies in the Reformed churches.

L'Eglise et Liturgie has also influenced liturgical developments in the Reformed Church in France. Despite the influence of Bersier, the liturgical situation there had been almost as chaotic as that in the Netherlands. Ever since Napoleon restored the Reformed Church in France it had had no fixed liturgical usage. The Genevan rites lingered long, but they never had official standing. It was only in 1946 that a commission was appointed to prepare a liturgy for the church.

The course pursued by this commission is somewhat parallel to that followed in the Netherlands. A provisional liturgy was published in 1950. But since the French Church is smaller and less diversified theologically than the Dutch, it was possible to revoke the provisional character in 1955 and give it official approval as the liturgy for use in the church. Although it, too, provides a variety of materials for confession of sin, intercession, thanksgiving, and so on, there is not the same theological variation as in the *Dienstboek,* nor is any variation allowed in the order of service. Most significantly the French *Liturgie* returns to Strasbourg. The Eucharist is indicated as the normal Sunday service; its omission as the irregular and abnormal.

Meantime, things have not been quiet on our own continent. To the north, our neighbors in Canada have been busy. The United Church of Canada possesses a splendid *Book of Common Order,* an interesting fusion of Reformed and Anglican elements, but has a committee at work on its revision. The Presbyterian Church in Canada similarly is in the midst of revising its own *Book of Common Order;* a first draft appeared in 1960.

In our own country the Presbyterian churches have approved a new *Directory of Worship* and are now working on the book of worship to accompany it. The Reformed Church in America issued the first volume of a *Provisional Liturgy* in 1958. It is now in the midst of a five-year period of study and trial usage.

Merely to list the accomplishments of the past twenty years is impressive. Beginning with the Scottish *Book of Common Order* in 1940, we have had the *Liturgie* of the Canton of Vaud in the same year, that of the church in Geneva in 1946, the *Book of Worship* of the English and Welsh Presbyterians in 1950, the *Dienstboek* of the Dutch Church, the *Liturgie* of the French Church and that of the Bernese Jura, all in 1955, the new *Directory* of the American Presbyterians in 1960, to say nothing of the various liturgies in progress in this country and Canada. Probably there are others.[21]

Fifty years ago many of these same churches had no liturgy at all, or at least no liturgical interest. Obviously we have been living in the most creative period liturgically in the long history of the Reformed churches. But what does it mean? How shall we interpret it? Should we fear it or welcome it? Above all, how shall we use it?

V

TOWARD A REFORMED LITURGIC

The reader's attention is directed to the title of this chapter. It is not "Toward a Reformed Liturgy." Many people seem to expect that any book on the worship of the Reformed churches should conclude with a specimen liturgy for the Reformed church, either a mosaic with bits and pieces of Reformed church liturgies from all over the world nicely fitted together, or something drawn from the author's ideals. This book will not be concluded in that way.

Our final search will not be for a *liturgy* but for a *liturgic*. That is to say we shall examine some of the factors which any order of worship for any Reformed church must take into account, whether that order of worship be part of an officially produced prayer book for an entire denomination or simply the service which a local minister is planning to use in his congregation next Sunday. Not only are there certain fixed factors to which the worship of the Reformed churches must always be responsive, but the implication of these factors changes with the times. Our task, therefore, will be not only to isolate these factors but to seek for their implication in our time and situation.

The conclusion of our study in this way rather than with a specimen liturgy must not be put down to the author's unwillingness to commit himself. He is simply seeking to be Reformed, loyal to what could be called the basic principle of Reformed worship. That principle asserts that there is not and cannot be one liturgy for the Reformed church, valid at all times and in all places.

We do not have and, if we are true to ourselves, we shall never have a Reformed Mass that will be identical in Amsterdam, Geneva, Edinburgh, Grand Rapids, Pittsburgh, or Charlotte, to mention some of our religious centers. Nor, one hopes, shall we ever see the production of a Reformed *Book of Common Prayer* undertaken by the Alliance of Reformed Churches. That kind of liturgical uniformity simply is not within the genius of the Reformed churches.

All that we have or ever can have in Reformed liturgics is the response of the congregation to the gracious and redeeming act of God in Jesus Christ. The form of that response can never be finally or universally fixed. It would be a most unreformed result if any of the liturgies mentioned in the last chapter should ever become canonized.

Though its patterns vary according to time and place, however, this response of the congregation must always be conditioned by attention to certain factors. The particular aspect of these factors, even their immediate content, will change. We have seen in the story up to this point how they have changed. But in spite of their changing relevance these factors remain the criteria by which our worship must be ordered and judged.

The Biblical factor is, of course, the primary one in Reformed worship. That sounds so obvious that one may wonder why it needs discussion. But its very obvious character may make it almost meaningless. After all, do not all ways of worship from the Roman Mass to the Quaker meeting claim Biblical sanction for the way in which they do things? Yet, as we have already noted, it is the Biblical factor which, more than any other, has been responsible for the modern liturgical revival in our churches, as well as in almost every other church in the world.

We must face the fact that there was a time in Reformed tradition when, liturgically speaking, the Bible was badly abused. It was used as a liturgical handbook if not as a liturgical textbook. The commonly accepted proposition in Reformed circles was that the Scriptures provided specific and precise directions for the conduct of public worship. One would think that completely opposed liturgical traditions, each claiming scriptural sanction for their practices, would have given some pause to those who held this theory, but that never seems to have happened.

For many years the idea appears to have been completely accepted in Reformed circles that nothing should be allowed in public worship but what was explicitly commanded in the Bible. With the results of that theory we are all familiar. The exclusive use of the psalms in praise, the banning of organs and musical instruments, the destruction of all forms of Christian pictorial art, the virtual reduction of worship to a sermon—these became the chief hallmarks of Reformed worship. And while we have, of course, become much less certain about most of these old standards, we have really ignored the basic liturgical questions raised by the Bible.

It is the Biblical factor itself which today is asking the Reformed churches whether they have not perverted the Biblical witness in their worship. Our basic perversion goes back to the beginning of our history. It was present in the thinking of Zwingli, but it was fully developed in later centuries. In all of its phases, orthodox, liberal, and pietist, Reformed church worship has at least flirted with an unbiblical dualism, an attempt to oppose the spiritual to the material in worship. For centuries the favorite liturgical proof text in the Reformed churches has been St. John 4:24, exegeted, as the scholars agree, in a most unfortunate way.

Whatever appealed to the mind, whether an orthodox dogmatic discussion or a liberal ethical essay, was *spiritual*. Whatever appealed to the senses—color, light, line, movement, or physical object—was *material*. Almost from the beginning, Reformed worship has been intellectualized. It is not surprising that many people in the Reformed churches are attracted by the Quaker way of worship. It is only the logical conclusion to a tendency which has always been marked in Reformed worship, a dichotomy between the spiritual and the material, the exaltation of the spiritual and the debasement of the material.

No one need spend time in understanding the historical reasons for this reaction if he knows anything about the worship of the late Middle Ages. But the Biblical factor asks whether the reaction has not landed us in a position which is just as untenable as the one from which we fled. The reconstruction of Reformed worship must begin here. We must recognize that this dualism is false and unbiblical. Not only is it inconsistent with the Biblical view of man, it is still more glaringly inconsistent with that cornerstone of the Christian faith, "the Word became flesh." Leaving to one side the fact that in any commonsense attitude there is as much of the material involved in preaching as there is in the Sacrament, a purely *spiritual* worship, in the common Reformed sense of the term, is impossible in a religion centered in the Incarnation.

The recovery of this Biblical insight, stimulated by a renewed scholarship of the New Testament congregation, should bring us back to the conviction which we would never have lost had Zwingli not conquered Calvin in our liturgics. In the act of Christian worship, Word and Sacrament belong together. Any attempt to set up an antithesis between them is completely false to the Biblical witness. They belong together not as successive or even complementary acts. They are aspects of a single whole. Word and Sacrament are only different media for the same reality, Christ's coming into the midst of his people. Dietrich Ritschl puts it in this way:

> The two are not to be set over against each other, for that would mean that the same Jesus Christ gives Himself to the members of His body in two different ways. Nor is it possible to say that the "action" of the Lord's Supper is the visible Word of God, as distinct from the invisible Word in the sermon. The usual term "Word and sacrament," quoted so often in our Protestant churches, is in fact without any Biblical support. It is the one life-giving Word of God that is present in both the sermon and the Supper.[1]

But, it may be asked, if this be true, if Word and Sacrament are both the same, coming of the same Christ, why are we not justified, as the Reformed churches have generally done, in taking one and, if not rejecting the other, relegating it to an obscure corner? We must be grateful indeed to the Reformation for the recovery of the Word. We know what its loss had involved. Divorced from the Word, the Sacrament soon becomes a kind of magic, a religious rite through which man can in some way manipulate and control the favor of God.

Surely it cannot be without significance that one of the great movements in the liturgical revival in modern Roman Catholicism is just an attempt to recover the Word. Centuries ago the reformers saw with devastating clarity what had happened. That accounts for the vehemence with which they insisted upon the restoration of the Word to its rightful place in worship. We must be grateful to them even for their vehemence.

But before we go on to consider the place of the Sacrament, we owe to it our heritage to ask whether the Reformation's recovery of the Word is something we dare take for granted in our Reformed churches. There are places in which it is being challenged, as witness the increasing popularity of the Eucharist, without the Word, as a kind of opening curtain for all kinds of conventions and assemblies, to say nothing of the kind of introspective devotions popular at summer camps.

But even if this kind of thing is more than marginal, it is not the real challenge. The real challenge is in that very aspect of worship on which we of the Reformed tradition have always prided ourselves, the sermon. To what extent do we still conceive of the sermon as a direct mediation of the presence of Christ with his own, a living Word spoken by him through the lips of his servant the preacher? And to what extent have our sermons become words, explanations of theology, expositions of the Bible, ethical discourses, psychological pep talks, religious meditations, commentaries on current events?

Make no mistake about it. We shall never be able to move toward a Reformed liturgic until we understand the Word of God ministered by the mystery (one could almost say *sacrament*) of preaching. That was the central thrust of the Reformation liturgic. If we lose it, we shall not have much left in the way of worship. If the sermon is merely human speech and the Sacrament a fellowship meal of remembrance, where is the vertical in our worship?

It would be imprudent to do more than ask to what extent that has already been the fate of Reformed worship. But certainly the reason for our empty pews is here. We have convinced our people that nothing happens in church. And nothing can happen if we no longer believe that the preaching of the Word is one of the ways, and in most of our worship the only way, in which the living Lord comes to be with his own.

But now do we need the Sacrament as well every Sunday? For we have to admit that in their violence in restoring the Word to worship the reformers came perilously close to eliminating the Sacrament. They did not intend to. There were all kinds of historical reasons and justifications for what they did. But practically speaking, what did the Reformed Reformation come to but the elevation of the Word as the norm of worship, the removal of the Sacrament to a place of neglect and insignificance?

We can have no sympathy with those who argue that this elimination of the Sacrament from the normal pattern of Sunday worship has deprived the Reformed churches of any real communion with Christ in their worship. That attitude betrays a total lack of understanding of Christ's coming in his Word. The Christ who comes to us through the preaching of the Word is the same Christ who comes in the Eucharist. His presence in the Word is no less real than in the Sacrament. Obviously it is not possible to speak of degrees of Christ's presence. The whole Christ is really present with his people in the preaching of his Word. The Reformed churches could not have been nourished for more than four centuries if there had not been a real presence in their worship.

But granting the full reality of Christ's presence in his Word, we have to ask ourselves whether by our neglect of the Sacrament we have not lost as much as the medieval church did by its neglect of the Word. For one thing, that loss of a real understanding of the Word which is such a threat to the life of the Reformed churches is in part the result of our neglect of the Sacrament. Could we so easily have dissolved the Word of God, that concrete and real event, into a set of general abstractions true for all times and places if every proclamation of the Word had been followed by the concrete and real event of the breaking of the bread?

And there are further questions to be asked. Would the preaching in the Reformed churches have become so loosely connected with the gospel, as it has in some places at least, if every Sunday it had been followed by the proclamation of the Lord's death till he come? Or could the Reformed churches have proved such fertile soil for the growth of sectarianism, producing one schism after another in their history, if every week they had reminded themselves that "we being many are one bread, and one body: for we are all partakers of that one bread"? It cannot be denied that of all the confessional groups in Christendom, we Reformed have shown the greatest tendency to fissiparity; the one thing about which we have had no conscience has been schism and secession. But we have been slow to explore the connection between this unhappy tendency and our intellectualization of the gospel, symbolized by our neglect of the Sacrament.

The question which the Biblical factor asks is simply this. A church that loses the Word must finally lose the Sacrament. But is it not equally true that a church which loses the Sacrament must finally lose the Word?

And how shall we reply? We are a church under the Word. We are the church which boasts that Scripture and Scripture alone determines its life. Then the time has come for us to bring our liturgical life under the scrutiny of that Word. It may mean sacrificing some of our most cherished liturgical practices and traditions. But least of all people can those who are Reformed countenance the idolatry of tradition.

When we bring our liturgical practice under the judgment of Scripture we cannot escape the fact that Word and Sacrament together form the way in which Christ meets his people in worship, that it is dangerous to seek to dispense with either the pulpit or the Table. Even though the whole weight of contemporary Biblical scholarship, no matter what the private faith of the scholar, re-enforces this conclusion, it is still possible to find some within our fellowship who refuse to accept it.

> The fiction that every true act of worship must be a communion service to which liturgy and preaching serve as merely a more or less incidental introduction is born from the Roman mass and in evangelical circles has long since been set aside by the facts.[2]

If by that statement the author seeks to reject the devaluation of preaching at the expense of the Sacrament, he is right. But if he is seeking to establish the priority of pulpit over Table, he is indulging in what could be called "Reformed mythology." They belong together as dual manifestations of one and the same Word.

Certainly there are all kind of practical difficulties to be faced in the restoration of the Eucharist to its rightful place in Reformed worship. They cannot be solved in a general way but must be worked out in local situations. Obviously the worst method of restoration would be simply to announce that beginning next Sunday the Lord's Supper will be celebrated every week. There must be careful preparation, patient instruction, and, above all, preaching which by its own sacramental quality mediates that presence of Christ which demands the confirmation and sealing of the Eucharist.

There is nothing to prevent an increased number of celebrations in a short time. This can be done simply by increasing the number each year from four to six, or six to eight, or eight to twelve as the case may be. Or there is much to be said for marking the great dominical feasts of the Christian year, Christmas, Easter, Pentecost, with celebrations in addition to the quarterly ones. Certainly all of our denominational liturgical commissions could be of great help at this point if in future liturgies, following the example of the *Liturgie* of the French Church, they were to indicate that the service of the Word without the Sacrament is the exception and not the rule.

But attention to the Biblical factor in liturgics brings us to a second conclusion. When we study the classic liturgies of the Reformation, especially those for the Eucharist, we can see that by dwelling almost exclusively on the Crucifixion and Atonement, they lack the note of thanksgiving and joy. There is very little *eucharistia* about them. Calvin's liturgy is something of an exception with its stress on the mystical union, but even so it does not give much evidence of the true Eucharistic note. Small wonder that in the post-Reformation era the Lord's Supper in the Reformed churches became a sorrowful and even gloomy event, a little Good Friday. In some parts of the Netherlands it was even the custom to attend the annual Communion in mourning. We have not lost this trait. Many a Reformed or Presbyterian congregation would find a Christmas or Easter Communion almost a contradiction.

There is some evidence that many of the Reformation liturgies were influenced by late medieval manuals of private devotion with their heavy emphasis on the crucifixion. Whether or not that be true, we are increasingly learning that Biblically speaking the true note of the Eucharist is not sorrow or penitence but joy, the joy of those who sit together with their living Lord and conquering Redeemer.

And it is imperative that in our Reformed liturgies we recover this Eucharistic joy. For the Christ who comes is the risen and living Lord who was crucified, not the crucified Christ who also rose again. Certainly the cross belongs in the Eucharist, especially in the Pauline accounts of it. But the Apostle put it there as a corrective to a joy that was becoming irresponsible hilarity. The basic note at the Table is joyful fellowship with the living and conquering Saviour. The church was right in calling this Sacrament *eucharistia*. Oscar Cullmann's words are appropriate:

> Christians will not rediscover the spirit of the first believers except on condition of assembling for the Lord's Supper in the joyful expectation of eating with Christ while they eat with their brethren, and of recalling once more that the Lord's Supper in the early Church was a feast of the Resurrection. The bold prayer, "Lord, come! *Maranatha!*" ought to assume again the eucharistic reference that it originally had, and it should express the double desire, which was realized for the early Christians, of seeing Christ descend into the midst of the faithful gathered in His name and of discovering for themselves, in that coming, an anticipation of His final Messianic return.[3]

A third relevance of the Biblical factor involves the order of events in the service. Of course the Scriptures do not provide us with an order of worship. But the Biblical accounts of the institution of the Supper, all of which have a liturgical ring about them, indicate certain specific actions taken in the upper room by our Lord on the night in which he was betrayed. They include the taking of the bread and wine, the blessing, the breaking, the giving, and the eating and drinking. A comparative study of the

historic liturgies of Christendom will reveal that while the widest
latitude is allowed in the rest of the service, at this point they
are alike in what they do. For this is part of our human obedience
to his command, "Do this."

A true Reformed liturgic will seek to preserve at the Table
what Dom Gregory Dix in his great book has called the "shape of
the liturgy." First there must be the taking and setting apart of
the elements. Because this action became associated with the
offertory in Roman Catholicism and because the offertory smacked
of sacrifice, the Reformed churches have largely forgotten this
action in the shape of the liturgy. In some parts of the Church of
Scotland, however, it has been marvelously preserved in the procession of elders who bring the elements to the Table, often to
the singing of the 24th Psalm, "Ye gates, lift up your heads on
high." Various experiments with the offertory procession also provide possibilities, although the action may be nothing more than
one done by the minister's speaking a few simple words. But it
ought not to be omitted.

The second action requires a prayer of thanksgiving and
blessing. It is strange how many people in the Reformed churches
suppose that all that is necessary for the Eucharist is the repetition of the words of institution from the upper room. While they
may of course be included in the prayer, in many of the historic
Reformed liturgies they are not even part of the Eucharistic service but are read before it begins as the warrant for what is to
follow.

In liturgical history this prayer has assumed a variety of
shapes, some very extensive, some extremely brief. Liturgical
scholars have isolated various parts of it, thanksgiving, anamnesis
(remembrance), epiclesis (invocation of the Holy Spirit), obla-
tion, and so on. Some have even tried to insist that the prayer is
not "valid" unless it includes one or more of these elements. Certainly it is good to pay attention to the ways in which this prayer
has been constructed in historic liturgies and the elements which
it has included. But when we go back to the earliest Christian
liturgical records, it becomes obvious that the only content on
which we can insist is that of thanksgiving and blessing. It should

be that kind of prayer; not one in which we stress our own condition, but one in which we joyfully glorify God for his wondrous love.

The remaining three actions are almost self-explanatory. In these days of little cubes of bread there should be at least one piece large enough to be broken, and in these days of individual cups one cup large enough to be lifted. And certainly, the eating and drinking by all present should underscore the fact that the Eucharist is the feast of the whole family of Christ, not a private meal for a few select spirits. It should always be the principal act of the whole congregation, not a peripheral event in the schedule of worship.

A Reformed liturgic must also be responsive to what could be called the Reformed factor. Obviously that means that our liturgies must express those insights which are part of our theological inheritance. Cultus must express creed. Perhaps this needs to be said in our time when there is a good deal of promiscuous and uninstructed borrowing which results in liturgical expressions that are not always consonant with our theology.

The hymnbook is the place where most of this happens. How many Presbyterians realize, for example, when they sing this stanza of Athelstan Riley's great hymn, that they are directly addressing the Virgin Mary?

> O higher than the cherubim,
> More glorious than the seraphim,
> Lead their praises, Alleluia!
> Thou bearer of the eternal Word,
> Most gracious, magnify the Lord,
> Alleluia! [4]

The Reformed theologian who studies the average hymnbook in use by one of our congregations could start enough heresy trials to keep him going a lifetime.

But there are other things which the Reformed factor in liturgy says, and not the least of them is this. Our liturgical life must witness to the priesthood of all believers. Worship is never the task of a special class, to be performed by them while the congregation simply sits and watches. It is the corporate task of the entire Christian fellowship. That is one of our principal Reformed emphases.

In passing we should note that the Reformed insistence is on the priesthood of *all* believers and not, as is so generally supposed, the priesthood of *every* believer. Too often this Biblical principle, recovered for us by the Reformation, has been mercilessly individualized with the tragic result that church, sacraments, worship, and ministry have become unnecessary since every man is thought to be fully able to come to God all by himself.

What the Reformed factor wants to say to us here is that worship is the responsibility of the entire Christian congregation, the whole *koinonia*, which is the body of Christ. As members of this holy people we have a liturgical responsibility together, whether it be in terms of adoration, prayer, and praise, whether it be in the ministry of proclamation, or whether it be in the ministry of service and love. The liturgical life of the Reformed congregation is not a matter of individual needs but of the witness and responsibility of the entire fellowship.

We must admit that that factor, so strongly implicit in the Reformed view of things, has usually been more honored by us in theory than in practice. If the evidence can be trusted, that has been true from the time that Zwingli conducted a monologue in the presence of a completely silent congregation. Nor did many of the later Reformed liturgies provide much of anything as the responsibility of the congregation, except for the singing of psalms and hymns. In our time even that is being taken away from some congregations and given to the choir.

There are some serious questions which we must ask ourselves here. How much better is the congregation that listens to a liturgical performance almost completely dominated by minister and choir than a medieval congregation which watched a liturgical performance almost completely dominated by priest and singers? No Reformed liturgy is truly Reformed which does not make a large and adequate place for the exercise of the priesthood of all believers in corporate prayer, praise, and affirmation as the people of God respond to the life-giving Word of their Creator and Redeemer.

It is a healthy sign that in all of the newer liturgies of the Reformed churches, especially those from the European churches, this is being done to a much larger degree. Both the French and Dutch liturgies, for example, contain congregational responses to almost every part of the service. In fact, the Dutch *Dienstboek* even prints the musical settings for these responses with the liturgical text. Such service books are really *liturgies*, providing for the work of the people. We need to think of our service books in this way and not as manuals and guidebooks for the minister only. It is perhaps worth noting that with the exception of a few Presbyterian congregations it is only in some of the Dutch Reformed congregations and those of the United Church of Christ (German Reformed) that liturgies are found in the pews. But why should they not be, if the people are to exercise their ministry to the fullest?

Too often, however, when we think about corporate participation in worship we think only in terms of those parts of the service which belong to the congregation—hymns, psalms, responses. But the Reformed factor will not let us stop there. It has some questions to ask about those things which we commonly think of as belonging to the minister—prayer, Scripture, and preaching.

Any discussion of the relative merits of free and liturgical prayer is unsatisfactory since the issue has become such an emotional one. In the Reformed pattern of worship it is a pointless one anyway, since from the time of Calvin our tradition has specifically made room for both. The Reformed factor in worship forces us to shift the question to a different level. Whether the prayers be free or liturgical, are they adequate instruments for corporate prayer?

We can admit that many liturgical prayers are not. Not all geese are swans! The mere fact that a prayer has been printed in a service book does not make it a fitting instrument for corporate worship. In many liturgical prayers the language is archaic. In many others the style is heavy and Victorian. Too many of the prayers in our liturgies are the result of striving after fine writing and poetic diction. Too many are concerned with pietistic, individual needs. All our American and British liturgies can profit from the French *Liturgie* in which the intercessions reveal creativity in both their content and their simple, direct style.

Furthermore even the finest liturgical prayer can be rendered useless by an inept minister. To string a series of liturgical prayers together without a scheme or framework results in something just as private as the most arbitrary free prayer. And too many ministers apparently feel that the fact that the prayers are printed in the book excuses them from the necessity of studying them before the service. The result resembles a high school boy trying to read Browning's poetry at sight.

But by a similar token there is a kind of free prayer which is equally unsuited for corporate worship. If it is not done in the great tradition (and there is a great tradition in free prayer), free prayer tends to become the minister's own private meditation done in public. Not only does it lack movement, eddying around one idea which is usually worked to death, there is no opportunity offered for the congregation to join in giving thanks and making intercession for all men. So anxious is the minister to exercise what he considers his ministry that he completely deprives his people of any opportunity to exercise theirs.

If it be replied that this kind of free prayer is more moving, more impressive, more helpful, the answer is that that really misses the point. Indeed, in a strange way it is a reversion to the very things against which the Reformation protested. For to say that a prayer is moving or impressive is to assume that worship is something done to us or for us by a holy man.

Whatever be the kind of prayer we use, the Reformed factor demands that we always keep before us the conviction that worship, including prayer, is something which is done by the redeemed community in expression of its Christian faith and responsibility. The corporate liturgy of thanksgiving must never be forgotten. The corporate ministry of intercession must never be neglected. This can be achieved by the great historic prayers of Christendom; it can be achieved by the free prayer of the minister; it can be achieved by the silent prayers of the people directed by biddings. That does not matter. What matters is that this part of the liturgy should not be pre-empted by one of the ministers as an extension of his sermon (or worse, of his personality) but that it should remain the common, corporate expression of the total ministry of all Christ's people.

What about the choice of Scripture to be read in the service? The Reformed factor in worship has a question to ask here too. In early days there was no problem about this in the Reformed churches. Entire books of the Bible were read and preached upon in continuous fashion. When he had finished a series of seventy-two sermons on Deuteronomy, the minister began a new series of forty-nine on Romans. There is more to be said for the custom than most of us are willing to admit, even though many of our congregations would probably weary of it.

But today we have a problem since the choice of Scripture is left entirely to the minister. This means that generally speaking the choice is determined by his homiletic intentions. In the old days, Scripture determined the sermon. We have very nearly turned the thing around and let the sermon determine Scripture.

But an even greater problem is posed by the fact that our system usually results in a distressingly small amount of the Bible's being read in the average congregation in any given year. Preaching often tends to cover a narrow range. Ministers often ride hobbies in their sermons. The result is obvious. And today when we have but one service a week in most places, and often but one lesson in that service, the situation is desperate, especially if we face the fact that that weekly exposure is the total acquaintance with Scripture that many of our people will have.

As Reformed churchmen we must be aware of the dangers attendant upon any attempt to bind the Spirit of God. But at the same time, for a Church of the Word to have in its public worship but one selection of Scripture chosen arbitrarily from a small selection of the favorite books or even chapters of one man is a situation which calls for correction. The use of the Bible in our liturgy must be more of a corporate matter than is the case at present.

There can be no prescribed recipe for achieving this. Dietrich Ritschl has made use of a small committee from the congregation, using this group in a joint working out of Scripture and sermon.[5]

Others will want to follow a lectionary, while others may be content with the general guidance of the sequence of the Christian year. Once again no Reformed liturgic can tell us all how it should be done, even though it insists that it must be done.

In addition to this insistence upon the corporate character of worship, the Reformed factor imposes on us the need to consider its eschatological character. This is more than a matter of liturgies which express an eschatological faith. It is surprising how few of the liturgies from the time of the Reformation do. Among all the classic Eucharistic liturgies of the sixteenth century only the Palatinate and Dutch forms show any eschatological concern. Our entire realization of the eschatological significance of the Eucharist is the result of contemporary rather than Reformation emphases, of an ecumenical rather than a Reformed factor.

What is at stake in this Reformed insistence upon an eschatalogical emphasis is the deep conviction that all liturgy must be provisional and transitory. It is this conviction that makes the task of Reformed liturgics a difficult one. Reformed tradition abhors a shrine, a fixed and permanent dwelling place of the presence of God on earth. Ours must always be a liturgy of the tabernacle, never of the temple.

This means in the first instance that we must refuse to accept any liturgy as final. There is no *right* way of doing things, nor can there ever be. But still more important, we must beware any attempt to enshrine God in our liturgical forms. In their worship the Reformed churches do not come to bow in adoration at the fixed abode of Deity. Their worship is a conversation, a dialogue, carried on between God and his pilgrim people. It must therefore always be changing as the pilgrimage moves.

When the Kingdom has finally and fully come, when *ta eschata* have been consummated, then we can speak in terms of liturgical finality. But in the meantime the church can never point to any liturgical form as the guarantee of the presence of God. Though written in a slightly different context, these words by Charles Hauter have a bearing here:

> If we consider Protestantism in this connection and if we review the consequences of the scriptural principle, we can say

that the difference from Catholicism is to be found in the fact that the scriptural principle implies a necessary refusal to bind the divine presence to any immanent thing. . . .

In this way of thinking, God can be everywhere or He can be nowhere, according to His own will. We cannot say that He is here or there. . . . The Christian idea of transcendence, as the scriptural principle affirms it, implies not only the promised reality of two worlds, but the freedom of the higher world to act or not to act.[6]

Certainly we are not in the realm of the completely arbitrary and unpredictable. We have the promise that where two or three are gathered together in the Name, he will be in the midst. The historic *votum* with which the classic Reformed liturgies began made this clear. "Our help is in the Name of the Lord Who made heaven and earth." Outside that Name, apart from that promise, there can be no worship and our coming together is a pointless exercise.

But at the same time none of our liturgical forms can in any way bind, ensure, or guarantee God's presence. We are not *in patria* but only *in via*. This is a factor which we must always bear in mind in our liturgical life and work. This is a factor to which we of the Reformed tradition must continually bear witness in the ecumenical discussions now going on about the liturgy.

But a Reformed liturgic must be responsive to the ecumenical factor. This factor has been operative in our liturgical life from the beginning. John Calvin certainly did not have his tongue in his cheek when he entitled his Strasbourg liturgy "A Form of Prayers following the usage of the Ancient Church." He was seeking to cut through all the accretions and distortions of medieval Latin worship to the tradition of the ecumenical church. We can agree that he was not entirely successful. From pressure, haste, and a lack of knowledge, he was not so well informed about the worship of the ancient or ecumenical church as we could have wished. But given his scanty acquaintance with the material, we must admit that he was extraordinarily successful in reaching the ecumenical heart of the liturgy.

Many of the efforts after Reformed liturgical improvement in later centuries also arose from an ecumenical concern beginning with Ostervald in the eighteenth century and continuing in the nineteenth with Bersier, Sprott, or the men of Mercersburg. As Calvin's ideal became less and less known and as Reformed churchmen came into increasing relationship with those of other traditions, most notably Anglican and Lutheran, the poverty of their own worship, to say nothing of its lack of continuity with historic tradition, became an embarrassment.

But it is in recent years that this process has been accelerated tremendously with the advent of the ecumenical movement. Beyond any doubt it is our participation in this movement that has been largely responsible for the great liturgical productivity in Reformed churches in recent years. While we have always respected it, in recent years we have been much more responsive to the ecumenical factor.

That does not mean, as some seem to fear, that we shall surrender our own Reformed tradition in worship. But it does mean that we shall not needlessly sunder ourselves from the liturgical tradition of ecumenical Christendom. Calvin preserved the historic shape of the liturgy for us. But in the violence of his time he rejected the whole treasure of liturgical materials in which that shape had been clothed. The ecumenical factor makes us see that in many ways that wholesale rejection was unnecessary and impoverishing.

Even as we have always joined the ecumenical church in repeating the Apostles' Creed, why should we not join it in singing the *Gloria in Excelsis* or the *Te Deum?* What is to prevent our preserving the great prayer of thanksgiving in the Eucharist or to join with cherubim and seraphim evermore praising God and saying "Holy, Holy, Holy"? The very real abuses of the Latin Mass, the only liturgy which Calvin knew, made it impossible for him to see the truly catholic and evangelical elements in it. But we have moved to a different perspective.

No one is advocating the adoption of any liturgical form because it is old or even because the majority of Christian people use it. But there is much in the ecumenical liturgical tradition which is perfectly consonant with both Biblical and Reformed requirements. Why should we further rend the body of Christ by refusing to join in worship with our Christian brethren of all times and in all places?

In any event, a study of the Reformed liturgies of recent years will reveal how they all have been enriched by materials borrowed from the historic liturgies of Christendom as well as the liturgies of other contemporary communions. The new *Liturgie* of the French churches in the Bernese Jura, for example, lists sources as varied as the Liturgy of John Chrysostom, Alcuin, Archbishop Laud, Rudolf Otto, and the Church of South India. Commenting upon the Eucharistic liturgy in this book, the editors have made an excellent statement of the significance of the ecumenical factor.

> The order of our liturgy for the Holy Supper is traditional and ecumenical. It gives us the privilege of joining again across the centuries in the eucharist of the ancient church, while helping us better to live the Holy Supper as a great thanksgiving in communion with Jesus Christ crucified and *risen* for us and in the expectation of His return of which the Supper is equally the pledge. This order also sets us in communion (though to be sure in widely different degrees) with those Christian churches which have maintained it uninterrupted through the years; Orthodox, Roman, Lutheran, and Anglican churches. Finally it specially contributes to the liturgical unity of the Reformed churches, being the order which almost all of these churches have adopted or are in the process of adopting.[7]

Doubtless there have been some instances in which the ecumenical factor has been used uncritically. There have been those in the Reformed churches whose feeling of liturgical poverty was so strong that they reached out anxiously to embrace whatever they could find without bringing it under the necessary scrutiny of the Biblical and Reformed factors. Such persons, if they still exist, need to be reminded that our liturgical poverty is not so great as they seem to believe, and that even if it were it would not excuse the uncritical employment of material from other traditions. But it would be tragic if such occasional mistakes on the part of liturgical enthusiasts should shut us up to the relatively meager fare of our own tradition, depriving us of the catholic heritage in worship which is just as truly ours as anyone's.

Ecumenically speaking, the time has come for us to recognize in what a significant position the Reformed churches are liturgically. Their Calvinist tradition binds them to the traditional shape of worship in Word and Sacrament. Unlike their brethren in some of the free churches, they have no need to stumble at this point, not if they face their tradition honestly and cease trying to justify its historical distortions. So far as the structure of liturgy is concerned, the Reformed churches are fully one with the ecumenical tradition.

But the Reformed churches have no particular form of words to which they are committed in the clothing of this liturgical structure. No Parliament has ever imposed a prayer book on them. No sovereign has ever gifted them with an Agenda to be followed to the last syllable. Their Biblical loyalty will always forbid their absolutizing any human form. Though their own liturgical forms may enjoy the sanctity of long tradition and rich association, they could scrap them tomorrow if they were persuaded that some other form would better serve to express the response of God's redeemed people. Where, as is often the case, they have no traditional form of their own, whatever in the ecumenical church is consonant with their Biblical and Reformed loyalties is there for the Reformed churches to enjoy.

In short, if the Reformed churches really understand their position, they have every reason for being liturgically fresh and creative. Bound by no tradition, obedient only to the Word of God, they have the chance to show how the ecumenical pattern of Christian worship can be used to express the response of man to his Creator in this twentieth century. No churches in the world should be less saddled with the traditional preoccupations, Victorian elegances, and lush ecclesiasticism which unfortunately still mar too much of their liturgical work.

There is one new insight which the ecumenical factor has brought us in which the Reformed churches have the chance to be especially creative. It is the close relationship between liturgy and mission. There was a time when it was fashionable for those who wished to discredit the liturgical movement in the Reformed churches to accuse it of medievalism and romanticism, of sitting in an ivory tower far removed from the real issues of life and death. Liturgists were depicted as intoning at their altars while the world around them was perishing. It was a favorite device to employ the familiar, if inaccurate, opposition between priest and prophet in Israel to give Biblical sanction to the accusation. Real Reformed worship was in the tradition of Amos.

Some of this criticism was probably deserved. The liturgical revival has had its romantics and antiquarians. But today this kind of accusation is as dated as a brass eagle lectern. For nothing is more in the forefront of liturgical discussion today than the close and inescapable connection between liturgy and mission.[8]

That connection can be described in two ways. First of all, the liturgy is the supreme act of public witness made by the congregation. There was a time in the ancient church in which the Eucharist was open only to believers. In the Orthodox churches it is still celebrated behind the iconostasis. But the historic reasons for this secrecy have long since vanished. In all of the Western churches, Roman and Evangelical, the entire service is public.

The entire liturgy, therefore, is an expression before men of the redeeming work of God in Christ. It is in the worshiping congregation that the world most obviously and most readily discovers the gospel. It is important that our liturgical life be an adequate expression of that gospel. When we consider the way in which so many of our services narrow the scope of the gospel, the introspection which has largely recentered our worship on our need rather than on God's grace and glory, we can begin to see why the missionary impact of the church in our time is disappointing. Too often our congregations are content to think that the missionaries to whose support they contribute relieve them of their own missionary responsibility. But the mission of the church comes to no more significant expression than it does in the liturgy of the church. Here is our public expression of the gospel. And here in that expression are both the motivation and the strength for our mission.

But in the second place this connection between liturgy and mission goes still deeper into the life of the church. Whenever the New Testament authors use one of the Greek words for *liturgy* (there are several beside *leitourgia*, all of them usually translated as *service*), it is difficult if not impossible to tell whether the reference is to an act of worship or to the larger responsibilities of what we so lamely call "Christian service." Sometimes indeed there have been rather sharp discussions between proponents of one or the other possibility.

But in the light of what the New Testament understands by *liturgy* the discussion may be pointless. In the minds of the authors of the New Testament there was no such distinction. The Christian *liturgy* was the total response of the body of Christ expressed in worship, obedience, and service. Our fatal blunder has been our effort to make a distinction here. Obedience and service that are not rooted in worship are as unthinkable in New Testament terms as worship that does not issue in obedience and service. Whenever we attempt to isolate these elements, we falsify the basic concept. There is but one Christian *liturgy*, focalized in Word and Sacrament, continued in mission and service.

That priesthood of all believers which the congregation exercises in its act of worship continues to be exercised as the members of the congregation go to their various stations in life, continuing to fulfill their apostolic mission, continuing the witness they have made together in worship.

The Reformed tradition caught a glimpse of this truth when it insisted that any vocation could be used to glorify God. But because this insistence was used negatively against the exclusive validity of the monastic vocation our tradition has never thoroughly explored its connection with the corporate vocation of the congregation in its *liturgy*. The Heidelberg Catechism provides another illustration of the way in which classic Reformation thinking approached the idea without quite realizing it. Its overall division is in three parts, the last of which is entitled "Of Thankfulness." This section includes both the Ten Commandments and the Lord's Prayer. In other words, the whole life of the Christian is an expression of gratitude, of thanksgiving.

But despite this profound recognition of thanksgiving or *eucharistia* as the basic motivation for the Christian life, the Catechism makes no attempt to connect this *eucharistia* with the *eucharistia* of the liturgy. The closest it comes is with the inclusion of Christian alms in its list of the necessary elements of worship along with the Word, prayer, and the sacraments (Question 103). All of the materials for the connection of liturgy and mission were present, but the connection was never made.

But now it is one of the chief concerns of our present situation to see that it is made. We have come to realize anew that apostolicity is one of the essential marks of the church, so essential that *church* and *mission* are almost synonyms. And that realization must now bring us to a fresh appreciation of the apostolic character of the liturgy. As the central point in our *eucharistia*, our glad and grateful response to God's redeeming act in Christ, the liturgy both informs and animates the whole pattern of that response as it extends from pulpit and Table into shop, school, and street.

This recovery of something which was close to the original mind of the Reformation we owe to the ecumenical factor. However it may be expressed in future liturgies for the Reformed churches, it must be one of the influential elements in the thinking of those who consider the question of worship. It is a sobering reflection that the liturgical scholarship of contemporary Roman Catholicism, though employing a somewhat different terminology, seems much more cognizant of the relation of liturgy and mission than much of our Reformed liturgics which still tarries with the aesthetics and psychology of worship. To take the ecumenical factor seriously is to find that it has something significant to say about worship here, something which is both Biblical and Reformed.

Once we go beyond general factors of this kind, we soon find ourselves in the realm of particularia for which any prescription is impossible. In such matters as ecclesiastical dress, the arrangement of the chancel, the use of lights and colors, tradition and usage have varied widely within the various churches of the Reformed family. This variety is part of what is involved in being Reformed. There is good Reformed precedent for the minister's being vested in cassock, gown, and bands; there is equally good precedent for his wearing street dress in the pulpit. There is good

Reformed precedent for the central pulpit; there is equally good precedent for the pulpit at the side of the Table. In the Reformed churches there can never be an absolute liturgical or ceremonial canon.

There have been, to be sure, certain things which the best Reformed liturgical tradition has always sought to express. These would include the organization of the liturgy in such a way that if Word and Sacrament cannot both be celebrated, the structure of the service will strongly suggest the Eucharist by placing the great prayer of thanksgiving and intercession after the sermon. Further to symbolize its Eucharistic character the minister should stand at the Table while he offers it. These basic things would also include the use of a general confession of sin together with a declaration of pardon. And certainly they must include the proclamation of the Word in every service, not merely its reading. That proclamation may be very brief, but it is an essential element in our worship.

But there is really only one liturgical canon in the Reformed churches. We must always be serious about our worship, Biblically serious, theologically serious, and in the best Calvinist tradition, ecumenically serious. Reformed liturgics permit no interest in worship that is merely pretty or pleasant. They are as chary of the suggestion that worship is here to impress man as of the notion that its purpose is to manipulate God. Reformed worship may be austere, but it is never frivolous.

And this great demand that we be serious about our worship in the Reformed churches means that we can never be content with it as it is. We must always be seeking the guidance of the Spirit that the congregation of the living Lord may offer to him and through him a more worthy sacrifice of praise and thanksgiving to the God of its salvation.

TO HIM ALONE BE GLORY

NOTES AND ACKNOWLEDGMENTS

CHAPTER I
A TALE OF TWO CITIES

1. Fritz Schmidt-Clausing, *Zwingli als Liturgiker*, pp. 88-122. Göttingen, 1952.
2. *Ibid.*, p. 117.
3. Quoted in P. F. Palmer, *Sacraments and Worship*, p. 157. Westminster, Md.: The Newman Press, 1955.
4. Walther Köhler, *Huldrych Zwingli*, p. 79. Leipzig, 1943.
5. Palmer, *op. cit.*, p. 246.
6. Schmidt-Clausing, *op. cit.*, pp. 128 ff.
7. *Ibid.*, pp. 88 ff.
8. *Ibid.*, p. 67.
9. The details of these revisions, as well as the text of Schwarz's first German Mass, can be found in Louis Büchsenschutz's *Histoire des liturgies en langue allemande*. Paris, 1900. There is also a good account of Schwarz's liturgy in W. D. Maxwell's *John Knox's Genevan Service Book*. Edinburgh: Oliver and Boyd, 1931.
10. E. Doumergue, *Essai sur l'histoire du culte reformé*, p. 21. Paris, 1890.
11. In making these outlines I have followed the practice of all liturgical historians in assuming that the Scripture lesson preceded the sermon, though it is not so indicated in any of the liturgies. In his recent book, *A Theology of Proclamation* (Richmond, Va.: John Knox Press, 1960), Dietrich Ritschl has challenged this assumption. It is his contention that the Reformers permitted no reading of Scripture in their worship but only the proclamation of the Word in the sermon. Cf. pp. 88-96.
12. Doumergue, *op. cit.*, p. 24.
13. E. van der Schoot, *Hervormde Eeredienst*, p. 74. The Hague, 1953.
14. A. Schlemmer and J. Cadier, *Le Culte Reformé*, p. 36. Montpellier, 1947.
15. Buchsenschütz, *op. cit.*, p. 106.
16. A. F. N. Lekkerkerker, *Kanttekeningen bij het Hervormde Dienstboek*, Vol. 3, pp. 187 ff. The Hague, 1956.
17. Doumergue, *op. cit.*, pp. 15-17.
18. *Ibid.*, pp. 43-44.
19. Stephen A. Hurlbut, *Liturgy of the Church of Scotland*, Part I, p. 30. Washington: The St. Albans Press, 1944.
20. Doumergue, *op. cit.*, pp. 334-335.
21. Lekkerkerker, *op. cit.*, p. 188.
22. August Ebrard, *Reformirtes Kirchenbuch*, p. VIII. Zurich, 1847.

23. Cf. Henry Harbaugh, *Creed and Cultus,* in *Tercentenary Monument,* p. 239. Chambersburg, Pa., 1863.
24. J. A. M. Mensinga, *Over de liturgische schriften,* p. 17. The Hague, 1851.

CHAPTER II
INTO THE SHADOWS

1. J. D. Benoit, *Liturgical Renewal,* p. 48. London: SCM Press LTD, 1958.
2. *Ecclesiastical Records of the State of New York,* Vol. II, p. 1240. Albany, 1901.
3. Luther D. Reed, *Worship,* p. 56. Philadelphia: Muhlenberg Press, 1959.
4. Ebrard, *op. cit.,* p. 290.
5. Mensinga, *op. cit.,* pp. 426-427.
6. *Ibid.,* p. 428.
7. Benjamin Engelbrecht, *Die Vrye Gebed en die Formuliergebed in die Reformatoriese Kerke,* p. 173. Utrecht, 1954.
8. Mensinga, *op. cit.,* p. 431.
9. J. H. Gunning, *Onze Eeredienst,* p. 57. Groningen, 1890.
10. *Ibid.,* p. 24.
11. *Ibid.,* p. 55.
12. Harbaugh, *op. cit.,* p. 282.
13. James I. Good, *History of the Reformed Church in Germany,* p. 325. Reading, Pa., 1894.
14. Harbaugh, *op. cit.,* p. 280.
15. *Ibid.,* p. 282.
16. Benoit, *op. cit.,* p. 35.
17. Eugène Bersier, *Projet de Révision,* p. xx. Paris, 1888.
18. Doumergue, *op. cit.,* p. 144.
19. James I. Good, *History of the Swiss Reformed Church,* p. 281. Philadelphia: Publication and Sunday School Board of the Reformed Church in the U. S., 1913.
20. Doumergue, *op. cit.,* p. 158.
21. Bersier, *op. cit.,* pp. xxvii ff.
22. W. D. Maxwell, *History of Worship in the Church of Scotland,* pp. 110-111. London: Oxford University Press, 1955.
23. Doumergue, *op. cit.,* pp. 231-232.
24. *Liturgie,* p. 403. Moutier, 1955.

CHAPTER III
THE GOTHIC AGE

1. J. J. von Allmen, *L'Eglise et ses fonctions,* p. 8. Neûchatel, 1947.
2. *The Liturgy, or Forms of Divine Service of the French Protestant Church.* Charleston, S. C.: Steam Power Press of Walker and James, 1853.
3. Bersier, *op. cit.,* p. xxxvii.
4. *Ibid.*
5. Doumergue, *op. cit.,* p. 153.
6. *The Liturgy, of Forms of Divine Service of the French Protestant Church, op. cit.,* pp. vii-xv.

7. Doumergue, *op. cit.*, p. 150.
8. Henri, Amiel, *The Journal Intime*, pp. 79-80. New York: Macmillan and Co., 1893.
9. G. W. Bethune, *Reasons for Preferring a Union with the Reformed Dutch Church*, p. 16. Philadelphia, 1836.
10. Andrew Bonar, *Presbyterian Liturgies*, p. 8. Edinburgh, 1858.
11. C. G. M'Crie, *The Public Worship of Presbyterian Scotland*, p. 328. Edinburgh: William Blackwood and Sons, 1892.
12. *Ibid.*, pp. 341-342.
13. G. W. Sprott, *The Worship and Offices of the Church of Scotland*, pp. 52-53. Edinburgh, 1882.
14. *Ibid.*, p. 118.
15. Benoit, *op. cit.*, p. 31.
16. Eugène Bersier, *Liturgie à l'usage*, pp. 3-5. Paris, 1876.
17. *Ibid.*, p. 49.
18. M'Crie, *op. cit.*, p. 354.
19. C. I. G. Stobie, *Another Wrestling Jacob* in *Church Service Society Annual*, No. 27, p. 23. Cupar, Fife, 1957.
20. Gunning, *op. cit.*, p. 148.

CHAPTER IV

THE LITURGY FINDS A THEOLOGY

1. S. J. Andrews, *William Watson Andrews*, p. 111. New York, 1900.
2. *Ibid.*, pp. 14-15.
3. Edward Irving, *Collected Writings*, Vol. I, pp. 605-606. London, 1864.
4. Townsend Scudder, *Jane Welsh Carlyle*, p. 71. New York, 1939.
5. The Catholic and Apostolic Church believed that before the death of the last of its Twelve Apostles the advent of the Lord would occur. The last apostle died more than sixty years ago. The community is waiting for further direction. But since no ordinations have taken place since the death of the last apostle, it becomes increasingly difficult to maintain the services of the Church. Those who are interested in this movement will find a good deal of information in *The Blinded Eagle* by Harry Whitely (London: SCM Press, 1955) and *The Catholic Apostolic Church* by Plato E. Shaw (New York: King's Crown Press, 1946).
6. David S. Schaff, *Life of Philip Schaff*, p. 178. New York: Charles Scribner's Sons, 1897.
7. Unfortunately I had written this chapter before the publication of James H. Nichols' *Romanticism in American Theology* (Chicago: University of Chicago Press, 1961). Those who wish to read not only the full story of the Mercersburg movement but a critical interpretation of it will find Dr. Nichols' book invaluable.
8. *Order of Worship*, p. 151. Philadelphia, 1866.
9. *Tercentenary Monument*, pp. 36-37.
10. Luther J. Binkley, *The Mercersburg Theology*, p. 52. Manheim, Pa., 1952.
11. Theodore J. Appel, *Life and Work of John Williamson Nevin*, p. 297. Philadelphia, 1889.

12. John W. Nevin, *Liturgical Question*, p. 23. Philadelphia, 1862.
13. *Tercentenary Monument*, p. 261.
14. *Ibid.*, p. 265.
15. John W. Nevin, *Theology of the New Liturgy* in *Mercersburg Review*, January 1867, pp. 43-44.
16. *Ibid.*, pp. 65-66.
17. *Tercentenary Monument*, p. 272.
18. Charles W. Shields, *Presbyterian Book of Common Prayer*, Supplement, p. 37. New York: Anson D. F. Randolph & Company, 1897.
19. G. van der Leeuw, *Liturgiek*, p. 156. Nijkerk, 1946.
20. van der Schoot, *op. cit.*, pp. 220-223.
21. If there are liturgical movements in the churches in German Switzerland and in Germany itself (as there may well be), I have no information about them. Hence their omission.
   One of the great Reformed churches of the world has also been omitted from the story, the Reformed Church in Hungary. The iron curtain has made it almost impossible to know what is happening there, save for the recent publication of a new hymnal.

CHAPTER V

TOWARD A REFORMED LITURGIC

1. Ritschl, *op. cit.*, p. 115.
2. Karl Müller, *Der Reformierte Gottesdienst*, p. 21. Neukirchen, n. d.
3. Oscar Cullmann and F. J. Leenhardt, *Essays on the Lord's Supper*, p. 23. Richmond, Va.: John Knox Press, 1958.
4. Athelstan Riley, "Ye watchers and ye holy ones," Stanza 2.
5. Ritschl, *op. cit.*, pp. 149-157.
6. Charles Hauter, article in *Foi et Vie*, Vol. 49, No. 1, p. 17. Paris, 1951.
7. *Liturgie*, pp. 410-411. Moutier, 1955.
8. Since this subject is new, there is not as yet a large literature. But a delightful and helpful introduction can be found in *Liturgy Coming to Life* by J. A. T. Robinson (London: A. R. Mowbray & Co. Limited, 1960).

BIBLIOGRAPHY
OF WORKS QUOTED

LITURGIES

"Liturge pour les paroisses de langue francaise," Moutier: Robert, 1955.
"Liturgy or Forms of Divine Service," New York: Anson D. F. Randolph & Company, 1853.
"Order of Worship," Philadelphia: Reformed Church Publishing Board, 1866.

ARTICLES IN PERIODICALS

Hauter, Charles. *Foi et Vie*, Vol. 49, No. 1. Paris, 1951.
Nevin, John W. *Mercersburg Review*, Jan., 1867.
Stobie, C. I. J. *Church Service Society Annual*, No. 27. Cupar, Fife, 1957.

BOOKS

Amiel, H. F. *Journal Intime*. New York: The Macmillan Company, 1923.
Andrews, S. J. *William Watson Andrews*. New York: G. P. Putnam's Sons, 1900.
Appel, Theodore. *Life of John Williamson Nevin*. Philadelphia: Reformed Church Publishing Board, 1889.
Benoit, J. D. *Liturgical Renewal*. London: SCM Press, 1958.
Bersier, Eugène. *Liturgie à l'usage des Eglises Reformeés*. Paris: Librarie Sandoz et Fischbacher, 1876.
Bersier, Eugène. *Projet de Révision*. Paris: Librarie Fischbacher, 1888.
Bethune, George W. *Reasons for Preferring Union with the Reformed Dutch Church*. Philadelphia: John E. Clark, 1836.
Binkley, Luther J. *Mercersburg Theology*. Manheim, Pa.: Sentinel Printing House, 1952.
Bonar, Andrew. *Presbyterian Liturgies*. Edinburgh: Myles MacPhail, 1858.
Büchsenschütz, Louis. *Histoire des Liturgies*. Paris: A. Couselant, 1900.
Cullmann, Oscar. *Essays on the Lord's Supper*. Richmond, Va.: John Knox Press, 1958.
Doumergue, Emile. *Essai sur l'histoire du culte reformé*. Paris: Librarie Fischbacher, 1890.
Ebrard, August. *Reformirtes Kirchenbuch*. Zurich: Meyer & Zeller, 1847.
Ecclesiastical Records of the State of New York. Albany: J. B. Lyon Co., 1901.
Engelbrecht, Benjamin. *Die Vrye Gebed en die Formuliergebed*. Utrecht: Kemink en Zoon, 1954.
Good, James I. *History of the Reformed Church in Germany*. Reading, Pa.: Daniel Miller, 1894.

Good, James I. *History of the Swiss Reformed Church*. Philadelphia: Heidelberg Press, 1913.

Gunning, J. H. *Onze Eeredienst*. Groningen: J. B. Wolters, 1890.

Hurlbut, Stephen A. *Liturgy of the Church of Scotland*. Washington: St. Albans Press, 1944.

Irving, Edward. *Collected Works*. London: Alexander Strahan & Co., 1864.

Köhler, Walther. *Huldrych Zwingli*. Leipzig: Koehler & Amelang, 1943.

Lekkerkerker, A. F. N. *Kanttekeningen bij het Hervormde Dienstboek*. The Hague: Boekencentrum, 1956.

Maxwell, W. D. *Outline of Worship*. London: Oxford University Press, 1938.

Maxwell, W. D. *History of Worship in the Church of Scotland*. London: Oxford University Press, 1955.

McCrie, C. G. *Public Worship of Presbyterian Scotland*. Edinburgh: William Blackwood & Sons, 1892.

Mensinga, J. A. M. *Over de Liturgische Schriften*. The Hague: Thierry en Mensing, 1851.

Müller, Karl. *Der Reformirte Gottesdienst*. Neukirchen: Buchhandlung des Erziehungsvereins, n.d.

Nevin, John W. *Liturgical Question*. Philadelphia: Lindsay & Blakiston, 1862.

Palmer, P. F. *Sacraments and Worship*. London: Longmans, Green & Co., 1957.

Reed, Luther D. *Worship*. Philadelphia: Muhlenberg Press, 1959.

Ritschl, Dietrich. *A Theology of Proclamation*. Richmond, Va.: John Knox Press, 1960.

Schaff, David S. *Life of Philip Schaff*. New York: Charles Scribner's Sons, 1897.

Schlemmer, André, et Cadier, Jean. *Le Culte Reformé*. Montpellier, 1947.

Schmidt-Clausing, Fritz. *Zwingli als Liturgiker*. Göttingen: Vandenhoeck & Ruprecht, 1952.

Scudder, Townsend. *Jane Welsh Carlyle*. New York: The Macmillan Company, 1939.

Shields, Charles W. *Presbyterian Book of Common Prayer*. New York: Charles Scribner's Sons, 1897.

Sprott, G. W. *Worship and Offices of the Church of Scotland*. Edinburgh: William Blackwood and Sons, 1882.

Tercentenary Monument of the Heidelberg Catechism. Chambersburg, Pa.: M. Kieffer & Co., 1863.

van der Leeuw, G. *Liturgiek*. Nijkerk: Callenbach, 1946.

van der Schoot, E. *Hervormde Eeredienst*. The Hague: Boekencentrum, 1950.

von Allmen, J. J. *L'Eglise et ses fonctions*. Neuchâtel: Delachaux et Niestle, 1947.

SUGGESTED ADDITIONAL READING

Good introductory books on the subject of Reformed worship:

Abba, Raymond. *Principles of Christian Worship.* London: Oxford University Press, 1957.

Brenner, Scott F. *The Way of Worship.* New York: The Macmillan Company, 1944.

Maxwell, W. D. *Concerning Worship.* London: Oxford University Press, 1948.

Micklem, N., ed. *Christian Worship.* Oxford: The Clarendon Press. 1936.

Nicholls, William. *Jacob's Ladder.* Richmond, Va.: John Knox Press, 1958.

Two books by W. D. Maxwell on the history of Reformed worship:

John Knox's Genevan Service Book. Edinburgh: Oliver and Boyd, 1931.

Outline of Christian Worship. London: Oxford University Press, 1936.